The Gentle Art
of Country Walking

The Shining Levels
Reflections on the Lakes
Lake District National Park (official guide)
A Visitors Guide to the National Parks of England & Wales
The Bliss of Solitude

THE GENTLE ART

ART

of Country Walking

John Wyatt

Illustrated by Pam Grant

CENTURY

LONDON SYDNEY AUCKLAND JOHANNESBURG

First published in Great Britain in 1993 by
Random House UK Limited
20 Vauxhall Bridge Road, London SW1V S2A

Random House South Africa (Pty) Ltd
PO Box 337, Bergvlei 2012, South Africa

Random House Australia Pty Ltd
20 Alfred Street, Milsons Point, Sydney, NSW 2061
Australia

Random House New Zealand Ltd
18 Poland Road, Glenfield, Auckland, New Zealand

British Library Cataloguing in Publication Data

ISBN 0 7126 5612 X

Photoset by Deltatype Ltd, Ellesmere Port, Cheshire
Printed and bound in Great Britain by
Mackays of Chatham PLC, Chatham, Kent

Contents

v

1

The Gentle Art – Why Walk?

Hurry is for slaves. Hurry breeds worry, worry ruins health and happiness. Hurry is the poison of the age. The guaranteed-to-cure antidote is leisurely country walking.

Country walking has nothing to do with hurry; it is freedom from all that nonsense, its pace is easy. The real and true art of country walking is not the cramming of miles into moments, but moments into miles. The secret is to have no concern about distance. Not to mind the length – but to feel the breadth.

The breadth of the experience is what counts. Country walking should open the mind and spirit; it is the discovery of the real living world, and in it perhaps something of yourself.

Country walking is available to anyone who can walk. It is not necessary to be an athlete, age is of little concern and families can walk together. The over-60s can country walk even if they have never been recreational walking before. It requires no expensive equipment, only a few basics, and it is the perfect, painless physical exercise.

To the country walker the countryside is not a race-track or a massive open-air gymnasium. Country walking is not jogging, competitive orienteering or fell-racing, and has nothing to do with long-distance hikes, enjoyable though these activities might be to some. It has little to do with sport, but all to do with recreation – moving at an easy, natural pace and enjoying the views and the countryside. To some a natural pace may be leisurely, to others vigorous – whatever comes easiest. But it allows plenty of time to stop and enjoy the objectives of the expedition – the stretching of experience; the unspoilt country, its sights, sounds and scents, and the tonic of breathing its clear unpolluted air.

Given that hurry is the disease of the age, by rejecting it one is part way to defeating worry. We are free human beings. 'All very well,' I can hear someone saying, 'but in the *real* world . . .' Yes, most of us are slaves to hurry, have to earn a living which often seems to mean running purely in order to stand still. But not, please God, for seven days a week. And that cliché about the 'real world': the real world? The real world is not made of concrete and brick and steel; banks and stock exchanges, factories and offices, engines and electronics, bank balances, debts and mortgages. Try as we may, in our sheltered artificial world we cannot tie off the umbilical cord which binds us to the real 'real world'. At long last we are beginning to understand what our ancestors were instinctively aware of aeons ago: that we are fellow animals living in interdependency on a life-sustaining earth. And we are also starting to realize that our existence is threatened by our 'real world' of unrestrained technology and the myth of the ever-expanding economy, of short-term gain, of getting and spending.

The true real world is probably clearer than we think. It is the natural world, or as near as we have to it, where the evidence of human activity is less obvious. It could be at the back door, but ideally it is where the sea meets the shore; where the rolling hills and moorlands have resisted the plough; where the mountains tell of time beyond knowing and where woodlands crowd the hillsides. It is the winding path before you, and the track hemmed with hedges; it is sunshine and moon shine, wind and rain. If you have no physical experience of these things, you have no touch with true reality.

Country walking is an expansion of horizons, but in much more than a physical sense. It is a widening of the horizons of the mind, an awakening from the sleep of repetitive, mesmerizing daily routine and its round of ritual – an awakening from that deadly sleep which dreams dreams, pretends that they are reality, and fears an awakening.

Our normal state is a kind of sleeping, from which the shake into a flickering wakefulness is comparatively rare.

The older we get, the more atrophied our senses become. The sleep of normality is cosy, wherein we can become less and less adventurous. The impressions of the countryside bombarding the senses from three dimensions (as distinct from seeing it on a television screen, or from the window of a car) might seem vaguely menacing, particularly if we have not shaken off the burden of the day's worries. How often do people admit that several days of a holiday have passed before they have unwound sufficiently to start to enjoy it? A waste! It is easy to learn to wake up, and the walk into the reality of the countryside is the best way. It could make every free day into a holiday.

Walking in the country can reawaken senses which we have forgotten we possessed. It can bring a glimpse of the infinite into the unused recesses of the mind, can stir the imagination to reach out to some awareness of a reality beyond the normal concept.

Take a walk up a hillside, relax, and look down at the bustle of humanity below. Then ask yourself – is it not a little absurd, this rushing about for no obvious purpose? Moving traffic coming from nowhere and destined for nowhere, going one way, and more traffic going in the reverse direction?

Country walking suggests new perspectives, and offers a fresh, clean view of life. Burdened by an unanswered question, taking it for a walk can produce the answer. Great thoughts are born of country walking, it is there that some of the greatest discoveries have their origins.

The countryside cannot fail to affect us. Peel away the tough outer skin of any born-and-bred thoroughly-urbanized and sophisticated citizen and you will find the weathered countryman. For only a few generations separate us from the pre-industrial revolution times when most earned their bread from the land. To think of the country-side as an extraneous environment is completely absurd – open your eyes to it and you have a long lifetime of interest. You cannot really see it from the window of a moving steel box! You need to step into it – and walk.

From the mere physical viewpoint, walking at a natural

pace is the purest exercise. It involves all the body's muscles and helps the circulation of the blood without putting undue pressure on the heart; it improves the action of the lungs and aids digestion. Taken regularly, it offers weight control and is a marvellous aid to a good night's sleep.

Disregard the nonsense which suggests that, to be beneficial, exercise must always test one to the limits. Have nothing to do with the man who scorns your four miles and says that you ought to do twenty. Punishing exercise is a penance for those who have a conscience about indulgence. Country walking is not a penance, it is a pleasure.

Do not assume that country walking necessarily involves climbing fells or mountains. High-level walking is specialized, and whether or not one aspires to the heights is a matter of personal choice. There are thousands of miles of public footpaths on offer: valley walks, village links, riverside and towpaths and shore-lines, abandoned railway lines, green lanes, ancient drover roads and pack-horse routes, woodland tracks and forest trails.

New landscapes, new horizons, the unexpected, a sense of adventure – they await all who are able to walk. Shake off the shackles, close the prison door behind you, step out into the countryside and there awaiting you could be undreamed-of freedom. You could be stepping out of an old life and into a new!

2

Footwear

Before seeking the new horizons, consider the basics. A country walker's main needs are simple: comfortable clothing and waterproofs, a map and the know-how to use it, and sensible footwear. These three; but the greatest of these is the footwear.

Think about this. There was a time when our ancestors walked barefoot on the land. As we now feel with our hands, so they felt through the soles of their feet. The earth was near to them, they knew its every wrinkle, every hardness and softness, every dryness and moistness. They knew it as their mother; it fed them, spoke to them. It was as near, dear and vital as the other elements – the free air, water, and fire. Today we have lost that intimacy.

We should of course try to reach some part of that experience, to walk barefoot, to regain that vital contact with the earth which was a necessity to our ancient ancestors. Perhaps those pioneers of human civilization knew at once through the soles and toes of their feet which earth was fertile, where water was near the surface, which land was so mysteriously special that it demanded reverence.

We have not only lost that nearness to the earth and the reading of the message it carries, but we miss the tactile pleasure – the coolness and the warmth, the softness, the grittiness, the hardness, the roughness. The springiness of pine needles. The sponginess of old leaf mould. The roughened striations of bed-rock. The dry roughness of pumice. The silk smoothness of glaciated volcanic. The rounded knobbly humps of limestone. The tingle of gravel. The searching ooze of mud, or the creep of sand. The rippling massage of fast-moving water. The tormenting titillation of dry dead bracken. The rough springiness of heather. The prickly bite of unexpected holly leaves. The coolness of moist grass and the warmth of sun-bathed rock.

In the comfortable, civilized way of life we deny ourselves much of our senses – the complex and beautiful way that our hands and feet are made; the articulated structure of bone, sinew and muscle, and the gathering of nerve endings. They are designed to touch and feel, to grip, to identify, to quantify. But by insulating our feet – those very sensitive members – from direct contact, we have halved the best tactile pleasures, for only our hands are now allowed direct access to our environment.

IMPORTANCE

Having said that, we have to remember the vulnerability of feet raised in footwear for many generations: the climatic coldness; the sharpness of flint and broken rock, the sting of nettle, the dangerous spines of gorse and thorn or, worst of all, the broken glass left by some mindless litter lout. Walking around known home territory is one thing – it can be pleasurable; it is worth an experiment. Try it! Stepping out into the unknown though requires protective footwear. Even our ancestors in pre-history presumably did their longer journeys wearing moccasins or sandals.

As country walkers, we can reach out again to a better understanding. But to step out into the real world, away from levels of concrete and tarmac, we must have sensible country footwear.

However what might, or what might not be, the appropriate country-walking footwear for a normal person is an involved and intriguing subject where there are no hard and fast rules.

If there was a society for the protection of cruelty to feet, it would proscribe most fashionable shoes. Many abuse their feet by cramming them into ill-balanced, ill-fitting, toe-trapping troughs. Tired and tortured feet affect one's whole attitude to life. Someone who is rude and ill-tempered might be nursing a stomach ulcer – or it could be that his feet are crying for mercy. Good comfortable footwear is essential: well-fitting for well-being. If you have

6

never enjoyed walking, it could be that you have never enjoyed using the right footwear.

Country walkers should be kind to their feet, so what should they wear? Some swear that they manage quite happily in Wellington boots, and I have seen them worn on the roughest mountain terrain. For short walks on wet ground they can be fine, but after a few hours of walking, the heat and perspiration they trap must build up to unpleasantness. I have yet to see a pair of Wellingtons fitted with safety-valves. Companions of 'Wellie-walkers' should be warned to stand well clear to windward when the wearer removes them. Wellingtons need not be ruled out for short walks if, and *only* if, they fit well over thickish socks; but even so, how to prevent the socks balling up and creeping down into the toes of the boots?

The right footwear for the individual depends upon how the feet are used. It is possible to buy the most luxurious and well-fitting footwear ever devised, yet to fall on your back after a few steps.

THE HUMAN WALK

The human walk is a fascinating and extremely complex process involving all the body's muscles and joints. The foot itself is a wonderful system of twenty-six bones, with attached muscles, cartilage and ligaments. Several times during each day the heel bone pounds the floor, the weight is thrown forward over the instep on to the ball of the foot, on to tarsal and metatarsal bones, and then the toe bones which hinge upwards to make the forward push.

Generally in a walking sequence one foot is lifted and moves forward and its heel is placed on the ground; then as the other leg and foot is raised, the first foot takes the weight. The body moves on and the first foot continues a rock forward to push off with the toes, at the same time as the second foot begins to repeat the process. That is what usually happens, but individuals display their unique variations.

How often have we recognized a friend at a great distance away by his or her walk? How a person places feet depends on so many variables such as body shape and weight, and inherited mannerisms. For instance, most turn their feet slightly outwards and the extent of the turn might determine the amount of weight placed on the outside of the foot and the degree of body sway. A sailor, once accustomed to balancing his walk on an unstable deck, spreads his walk outwards. Some people naturally take short, quick steps; some long strides. Some hammer the heel in hard, others push strongly from their toes. Some spring the walk upwards, others slide it. Then the placing of the right foot does not necessarily match that of the left; there is invariably a subtle difference. Because the movements are so complex, the range of characteristics is vast.

It would be absolute nonsense therefore to suggest that there is a magical type of footwear to suit all walkers. The general rule in choosing footwear must rely on the buyer's common sense. The foot, being an articulated structure, must not be held too rigidly if it is to function well. The heel and sole of the footwear protect it from impact and from the roughness of the ground. The heel of it takes the brunt of the ground strike, and should be thick enough to be suitably cushioned; the sole too should be substantial enough to be cushioned, but not sufficiently thick and stiff to affect the sequence of movement.

TYPES
A 'bendy' boot is fine for easy walking; something stiffer is required for rough terrain. As the push off is made from the sole, it should have a slip-resistant tread. The uppers should be flexible enough to bend to the movement, and to accommodate the spread of the foot as it takes the weight.

Beware of misleading advertisements. It is wrong to assume that a boot designed to take one up Everest can take one anywhere. Nor should it be concluded that the correct footwear must be expensive to be good.

Not all that long ago, serious country walkers would be wearing nailed boots. In a way I mourn the passing of nails and wonder if the lighter type will ever return. After all, lightly-nailed sandals were worn by the Roman armies of old and they tramped all around Europe! I was considered a strange eccentric because I was still wearing nails long after the fashion changed to the stout, moulded rubber soles. Colleagues on our mountain excursions used to warn their companions to keep clear of me when navigating as my 'hundredweight' of boot nails might deflect their compass readings!

In the past all country workers wore nails. As a lad, I was 'rigged' with nailed boots on the advice of my farmer neighbour when I got my first job in a forest. These were the 'shepherd's boots' still favoured by some northern hill farmers today, though they are rare now and expensive. Made of stout, greasy leather, they are boat-shaped (like wooden clogs were once made), with a well-nailed fore-and-aft curved sole so that forward progress is aided by a rocking heel-to-toe movement. The nails and the stout construction make such boots heavy – around 10 lbs or more.

However, it should not be assumed that the heavy weight of this type of footwear restricts progress. The swing of them produces a pendulum-aided rhythm to the walk, and momentum is considerably improved. It is all to do with the science of kinetics: point the boots in the right direction, start swinging, and away you go! The boots make a very satisfying 'clunk' as they bite into the earth. On cattle-market day it is possible to recognize the passing country worker brought up on shepherd's boots by his gait: long swinging strides, knees slightly bent, looking as if he knows precisely where he is going, his boots having for years firmly, enthusiastically and inexorably responded to his directive!

I know from experience that nails are superior to rubber on slimy rock and frozen grass slopes, when crossing streams, on new shallow snow on steep slopes (deadly in rubber soles!), and on frozen snow where rubber boots would need to be fitted with 'crampons' – virtually detachable nails! Nowadays nailed boots would have to be specially made, and their wearers would be labelled eccentrics, as I was.

Now rubber soles are the thing, though they have their

advantages and disadvantages. They vary in composition from soft to hard, but whatever – like car tyres – they need to have a good tread for maximum grip. They can be moulded in a manner popularly known as 'vibram', or they can be lightly studded; one type is better known as 'Klan'. The studded kind (Klets) were developed when Ken Ledward, an outdoor gear researcher, suggested that slips and falls were caused when the conventional treads picked up mud, clay and gravel and became virtually smooth soles. Not only were studs less inclined to become clogged, but environmentally they were better as they caused less wear on footpaths.

SURFACE HAZARDS

There is no such thing as the ideal type of footwear for every person, any more than there is one ideal type for every kind of country walking. For instance, over more years than I care to count I have made a personal collection to deal with the varied terrains. I have short light 'bendy' Wellington-type boots, with studded soles, designed for orienteering; these I use mainly for short walks in wet woods and low-level wetness. Then I have light canvas 'trainer' sports plimsolls with cushioned soles, ideal only for dry conditions at low levels (and the hard pavements of town). My very light studded rubber-soled boots with suede uppers and cushioned inner soles are absolutely superb on any terrain in dry conditions; while a pair of light leather boots, with studded rubber soles and cushioned inner soles, are good and comfortable in any conditions on most kinds of terrain except winter mountains. I have medium-weight leather boots, vibram-soled, for mountain walking on any conditions except snow and ice. And lastly I have very strong heavy-duty leather boots, also vibram-soled, for winter mountaineering only.

Of course one has to compromise. If I had only one pair of boots, which would I choose? I would go for light leather boots with cushion insoles (or 'footbeds') and real rubber, not plastic, soles. Once considered to be cheap substitutes for the stouter heavier walking boots, light boots are now of much better quality and have become the popular buy. The uppers can be soft leather, or part suede or part canvas. The first pair I tried were thrown at me from the back of a mountain-rescue Landrover on a night when I came upon a roadside crag rescue and was without equipment. I thought they were magic and was an immediate convert; however, I later found that such boots could be almost unmanageable on frosty ground.

One has to learn to adapt to the shortcomings of each type of footwear. Any type has limitations, and the secret of safe walking on rough terrain is to know those limitations and to be ready to take care in placing the feet.

There are at least ten main terrain hazards: (*1*) steeply sloping ground with wet grass; (*2*) similar slope with dry grass in hot weather; (*3*) a skimming of thin snow on steep ground; (*4*) snow in all its other varied forms from slush to rock-hard; (*5*) wet rock, particularly smooth rock, and even more dangerous, rock long wet and growing a film of algae; (*6*) frosty ground with visible ice, or more hazardous, invisible 'black ice' on rock; (*7*) loose stones or unstable gravel on slopes; (*8*) rocky fords across streams and rivers, or rocky sea-shore shallows; (*9*) slippery tree roots and logs; (*10*) mud, and cow pats!

PERSONAL CHOICE

I have repeatedly referred, by the way, to boots – not shoes. Ideally ankles need covering for their protection against stones and rock, and there is a need to prevent mud, grit or water from entering – as they will where there is a gap around the ankle. Footwear secured above the ankles is also less likely to slop about on the foot and raise blisters. The upper part of the boot around and above the ankles should be of soft leather; on some the cuff is padded.

Boots should be worn over substantial socks – woollen, or a woollen mixture, not nylon. 'Loop knit' type are good. Some walkers prefer to wear two pairs of socks – an inner, thinner pair perhaps, and an outer of thicker woollen. It used to be the done thing to wear two pairs of thick socks or

11

stockings, but nowadays boots are so well padded there is hardly that necessity.

Having said all this, there can be no firm rule except to wear something comfortable and sensible. When buying footwear some may choose to say a prayer to St Crispin, the patron saint of shoemakers, to ask for guidance, then go to a shop which specializes in outdoor equipment and offers plenty of choice. The shop-keeper will loan you some suitable socks to try the footwear over. Do not be satisfied until there is a good fit, not tight, and remember that feet expand when they get hot – maybe by as much as half an inch. (It might be a good idea to try on the footwear over two pairs of walking socks to allow for this.) If the fit is too slack, blisters will be raised. Footwear should not pinch anywhere, but the heel should be firmly gripped. The fore- and aft-fit is critical. Going downhill the toes are pushed against the boot front, and with too slack a fit the foot will slide forward to crush the toes.

For some people, like myself, the correct footwear width is hard to find. Imported boots are made on narrow lasts, presumably as the population of the country of origin has slim, elegant feet. The home product would be better for broad footers, though a number of good bootmakers at home and abroad offer varying widths. Ladies' boots should be made on ladies' lasts, whereas many are in fact made on less satisfactory scaled-down men's lasts. There is no way of telling except by trying for comfort, therefore it follows that ladies may need more time to be certain of a good fitting.

If in doubt when choosing between two pairs of boots at a fitting – go for the larger size for safety. Better too large than too small, and one can always wear two pairs of socks if necessary.

Be wary of being told that the footwear needs 'breaking in'. All boots need a settling period to feel thoroughly comfortable, but in a good fit, not a lot. (I suppose the exception is the acquisition of a heavier mountaineering boot, but of that more later.) A 'bellows' type tongue to the footwear is an advantage, as it prevents entry of water through the lace-holes; part canvas or suede uppers can be sprayed with waterproofing solution. The footwear should be reasonably waterproof, but one need not be obsessive about their being completely so. It used to be thought that a chill at best, and pneumonia at worst, followed wet feet as surely as night the day. However, so long as they are kept warm, damp or wet feet cause no such problems. Woolly socks can keep the feet comfortably warm even when wet. In some conditions water may slop over the ankles into the best of boots. Don't worry too much about it!

New footwear, like new companions, might seem strange on first acquaintance. Try them first on short walks. If you have chosen well it should be the beginning of a long-lasting friendship.

The correct boots or shoes should feel as comfortable at the end of the day as at the beginning. They are the walker's best friends and need friendly care. Leather should not be dried out too quickly; after a wetting and slow drying, they should be brushed and then treated with wax to keep them supple and water-repellent. This is done in a few minutes but can help them to last for years. I have known some who treat their boots with almost superstitious reverence. Boots adapt to the character of the wearer and develop a kind of personality of their own. They have their mystical as well as their physical side and have long been considered as good-luck symbols. There is the ceremony of boot-throwing at weddings, and sometimes shoes are tied to the back of wedding vehicles. Cinderella was found by her prince at a ceremonial shoe fitting, and Pythagoras and Augustus Caesar always insisted that it was necessary to put the shoe on the right foot first, or there would be dire consequences for the rest of the day.

For myself I would never consider condemning my outworn pair of boots to the indignity of a rubbish dump. They are old friends that have taken me on many adventures and I give them a Viking funeral.

And to rest feet at the end of the walking day? Wash them, and walk about indoors in soft slippers, in socks – or better still, barefoot!

13

3

Clothing

When Adam and Eve were banished from the Garden of Eden into the cold world, they were provided with coats of skins. Clothing was more than the symbol of lost innocence; it was a necessity. What made possible the human settlement of the globe from its Eden to the farthest polar reaches was the craft of tailoring.

Nowadays, to the urban human, clothing is more about style than function. Appearance might be an important consideration when acquiring town wear, for most people feel compelled to conform to a particular image. But clothing for the outdoors in the countryside has to be practical and comfortable; there the purpose of wearing clothing is to protect the body, to maintain its temperature, and to allow free movement. It can also look smart, of course, but that is the secondary consideration.

What then? The old Scottish drover who walked his cattle for long distances in all sorts of weather over open country, and often had to sleep outdoors, wore woollen trews, a woollen shirt, waistcoat and coat – and over all he wore his plaid. This was a large woollen sheet up to 18 feet long and 5 feet wide; to put it on he would lay his belt upon the ground and on the belt he would lay the plaid, folding it lengthwise and making pleats at the near end. Then he would lie down on it and lifting up the ends of his belt, he would fasten it around his waist. Standing kilted, supporting the upper plaid, he would then pull the upper length over one shoulder, wrapping it around and forward to be fastened with a bodkin. After putting on his woollen hat, he was ready for his long walk. So come rain, wind, snow or the fiercest frost, his protection was around 90 square feet of close-woven wool over woollen clothing. This would be the slightly oily, hairy wool favoured by countrymen and sailors.

Hill shepherds in old times, facing the extremes of weather, wore close-woven woollen coats over woollen underwear and shirts. In Cumbria the coat was made of the harsh undyed wool of the local 'Herdwick' breed, a type of wool now used for making carpets! The coats were sometimes waterproofed with pitch; the smell must have been . . . interesting.

Wool was the answer to all the weather problems faced by those of olden times who lived and worked in the great outdoors. When man first learned to spin and weave wool he was free to walk, sail and ride into all the regions of the world. The advantage of pure woollen clothing is that it still retains much of the body temperature even when soaked with rain. It also 'breathes', allowing body vapour to escape when things get too warm. The disadvantage of using even the best of it as outer clothing in persistent wet weather is that it eventually gets rather heavy! 90 square feet of plaid, even if hairy and oily, must have placed a burden on the drover's back; and how to dry it?

UNDERWEAR
Going more deeply into the subject: in cold weather choice of underwear is important. Modern thermal underwear of various kinds offers good protection, but some find it unpleasant and a build-up of static electricity can produce some startling pyrotechnics when discarding! Wool is the obvious alternative, though with memories of the prickly kind issued in the armed services some, like me, will be biased against it. (I swear it was the constant agonizing scratching that kept me warm in the North Atlantic weather.) Some are happier with silk, which they claim is warm in winter and cool for summer, but it's tricky to wash and retain shape. In dry summer weather pure cotton is arguably the best.

OUTER WEAR
Nowadays wool is no longer the only option for outer wear. With a much wider range of textiles to choose from when venturing into the open air, we can gratefully wear

15

whatever is right for the day, and carry light waterproofs in case of rain.

There is enormous competition in the manufacture and sale of outdoor clothing, and magazines catering for outdoor enthusiasts have regular articles on tests. Varieties are so prolific that the test results and recommendations are often more confusing than helpful. I once attended a gathering of authors of outdoor features where there was agreement in informal discussions on the special needs of clothing for country walking, but no agreement at all on what was the all-round best. Some manufacturers make exaggerated claims, some pander to fashion.

There are 'gear people' who make a lot of fuss about getting equipped with the best and latest in design technology for their leisure activity, whether it be walking, mountaineering, skiing, sailing, tennis or golf. Their skill in their chosen recreation is often in inverse ratio to their purchasing power; they are people who are more concerned with what they look like than what they will feel like.

The fact is that there is no need to go to great expense in acquiring outdoor clothing. What is required is an outer garment that is roomy enough to fit comfortably over inner clothing, is light, windproof, and possibly showerproof.

An anorak is the favoured outdoor jacket – in length not too short, or it will leave a cool gap at the waist (a 'bum freezer'). A full-length zip is an advantage, and in my opinion the garment should have good gusseted pockets, one of which at least is large enough to accommodate a map. Most anoraks are showerproof. Some are completely waterproof, which is all very well in bad weather, but in other conditions may mean that it could become uncomfortably hot inside. It is best to *carry* a light waterproof to cover all, of which more later in this chapter (*see* p. 18).

Some walkers prefer to have two anoraks – one with padded linings for winter and another for more temperate times – but there is no need to go to that expense. A light, roomy jacket can take layers of inner cloth in winter. Layers trap insulating air and have the advantage that they are adjustable; a layer can be removed or added if one gets too hot or too cool.

Most may regard it as a minor point, but some textiles are noisy! Those who are keen on nature photography, bird-watching, recording bird-song, or who just like to enjoy the luxury of complete silence – take note!

Trousers or breeches, reasonably windproof, are preferable to shorts and skirts. Unprotected legs can suffer among brambles, gorse and bracken; nettles are even worse, I can vouch for that! And if mosquitoes and midges favour you, particularly the vicious Scottish and Scandinavian varieties, unprotected limbs offer a free feast. Bare legs are for heat-waves in spine-less terrain, or the beach. Even then it is a good idea to carry a light pair of trousers to cover them in case of weather change or sunburn.

Some walkers wear light gaiters, normally worn for mountaineering. They are a help in tramping through heather and peat hags, and when wading through thorn scrub. A hat is a good idea, preferably one that can be folded up and pocketed when not needed. In hot weather a floppy-brimmed cotton hat is a protection from the sun and goes some way to keeping off marauding insects, especially if treated with repellent. In cold weather there is a great heat loss from a hatless head – a woolly hat, then.

In cold weather too one can be miserable without gloves. On a mountain expedition, a keen colleague of mine had to turn back after suffering considerably from the loss of his pair. It is a good idea to fasten a long tape on childrens' gloves, passing it through the jacket sleeves and around the back. In fact this is not a bad idea for absent-minded adults. If you come across an odd glove on a walk it might well be mine, one of many losses! Fingerless mittens are useful if there is a compulsion to seek the aid of the map repeatedly, also if you handle a camera. It is remarkable how well they keep hands warm as well as mobile. I have thin fingerless mitts which, if necessary, I can cover with gloves.

WATERPROOFS
Now for those waterproofs ideally carried in the rucksack in

case of rain. Some walkers swear that they are not needed if the everyday anorak is waterproof anyway, but the experienced will say that total waterproofs trap body perspiration and only become bearable when it is preferable to be warm and damp from the inside, rather than cold and damp from the outside.

So what is the best option? There is a temptation to buy the ultra-lightweight waterproof that can be folded and carried in a pocket. But *very* thin material is a menace; it clings closely, and totally seals out the air. Some ventilation is necessary and a loose fitting is essential.

My earliest wet-weather walking in youth was done in an ex-Army groundsheet/cape. This hung loosely, ideally offering plenty of ventilation between it and the inner clothing. Another advantage is that it covered my ruck-sack too. But in the wind it became unmanageable! I finally retired it as a walking aid when I all but took flight while struggling with a gale on the traverse of Striding Edge on Helvellyn. (The ravens riding the air currents may well have wondered, 'Is this a man or a bird?') The older type of cycling cape was once popular with walkers, and apart from the fact that it did not allow much freedom to the arms, first class! But here again parascending became a possibility.

From my own experience I would recommend a loose-fitting waterproof with a full-length zip protected by a flap and seams protected inside by tapes. The garment can then be put on quickly, and can be fully opened when necessary to allow for complete ventilation – vital! It should be long enough to cover the hips and should have pockets covered by ample flaps. Most come with a hood for protecting head and neck; a peak to the hood is an advantage to spectacle wearers. The one fault with hoods is that hearing is restricted, and in fact many waterproof materials produce noise with every move. You will miss the bird-song and, sometimes more important, the worry of approaching traffic if you are walking on a roadway. Ideally I think a jacket with a high collar is better, worn with a broad-brimmed hat – but not on the mountains in windy weather! The vulnerable area is around the neck; a scarf of towelling material prevents a water leak into inner clothing.

What colour? I raise this question as mountain-rescue spokesmen have often recommended bright colours, and waterproofs frequently come in shiny eye-dazzling red, yellow or orange. It is argued that in remote country lost people are difficult to find when wearing drab colours. As a mountain-rescue team member for many years, I can say that I have spent countless strenuous hours searching for lost people dressed in olive-green or khaki anoraks – sometimes at night; sometimes, if not invariably, in bad weather. Even so, at the risk of being labelled a crank, I must register an objection to bright colours in the country-side. Who wants to see sublime prospects spoiled by distant parties in screaming anoraks? I swear that walking parties so dressed can be vividly seen by the spy satellite cameras in outer space! Obviously it is a mistake to wear bright colours when visiting a nature reserve. Vivid-coloured waterproofs are for seamen and yachtsmen, in my opinion.

A waterproof jacket without waterproof over-trousers can be nasty. All the rain will run down to thoroughly soak the legs before entering the boots! So light waterproof over-trousers, ample enough to allow free movement, are also a necessity. They should have side zips long enough to open so as to allow them to be pulled over boots quickly without a struggle; they should also fit fairly close around the ankles, as looseness there can cause an accident! I once went to the aid of an elderly, long-experienced walker who had fallen off a rocky ridge. Luckily he had no broken bones. When I asked him what had happened, he groaned, 'I tripped over my (expletive) new over-trousers.'

It is possible for skirt or kilt wearers to acquire water-proof over-skirts.

A properly equipped walker can actually enjoy the rain. Hurrying in the rain through urban streets should not be equated with walking in the countryside, where all green things feed on the rain and breathe life.

First there are the scents. There is nothing to match the

zestful scent of a birch wood in an April shower, as it stimulates and cleanses the olfactory channels and lungs. It is the essence of catkin pollen and the fresh oil of new-breaking buds, a surging of life that is typical of silver birch, the great urgent rapid-growing colonizer of open land. Then there is the peppery smell of oak woods in a May shower, or in late autumn rain when the air is enriched with the scent of brown leaves and fungi. Flowers and blossoms of all kinds breathe their scents into the air after rain.

Only in the open is it possible to smell rock in the rain – quite subtle and impossible to describe. Amongst limestone there is the not unpleasant smell as the rain, which is always slightly acid, interacts with the alkaline. Granite has a hint of sulphur. Wet earth and clay has a scent of its own very local character; peat has a wild, rough, slightly oily smell.

And what is more invigorating than the salty shore-line smell of rain driven from the sea! Does it matter if it stings the face and touches the lips?

Then there are the sights. The most magical thing is when the sun breaks through and lights hanging jewels on trees, hedges and shrubs; and everything is shiny fresh. The colour of rock and stone can only be appreciated when wet, and it can give life to the architecture of a country church.

As Wordsworth said of enjoying the countryside, 'It is upon the mind which the traveller brings with him that acquisitions, whether of pleasure or profit, must principally depend.' If we let ourselves believe that rain is unpleasant then we are missing out.

ALL-PURPOSE WEAR

Some walkers will say that the ideal solution to outdoor wear is to buy outer garments of the magic new 'breathable' materials of man-made fibre, that allow body vapour to escape yet keep rain out. A garment for all seasons and all weather! Modern technology has invaded all human activities, even the informal recreational. Encountering the sales promotional material in an emporium devoted to outdoor clothing, one might be tempted to think, 'I would like to take up country walking but I can't afford the expense!' Yet to a normally fit person walking is the most natural form of activity and, I repeat, it really requires no great expense at all.

However, it has to be acknowledged that modern technology offers extra freedom and comfort for a price. For those who have money to spend and want the best that modern technology can provide, here are some details of the modern alleged 'breathables'. Firstly there is the plastic microporous membrane sandwiched between two layers of textiles, which allows the fine body vapour to pass through it, but sheds the larger droplets of rain. This needs to be kept clean as dirt can clog the pores. A second type is the 'hydrophilic' which is said to attract the passage of perspiration vapour to the outside, but repels rain.

Other types are being developed. You may have to take out a second mortgage to buy this equipment, but does it *work*? Many swear enthusiastically that it does, provided the inner clothing is such that it allows body vapour to 'wick' to the surface. This rules out cotton, so inner clothing has to be of man-made fibres or wool. Many hail the new materials as a great revolution; others are disappointed. I can only relate my own experience. I have had a pair of light over-trousers of microporous material and found them highly successful – so much so that it was possible to forget that I had them on. A second, cheaper pair was less successful and when wet smelt of cat pee. But the jacket? I have one which is very well made, with a tough outer material, but it is not a total success. Although I still enjoy wearing it, it is not completely waterproof against wind-blown deluge on the one hand and saturating Highland mists on the other. It can also be hot. One manufacturer of both jacket and over-trousers using the new materials admitted to me that the solution of dealing with body vapour in wet weather was still elusive. Possibly, he said, there will never be a real answer. Will someone invent a battery-operated air-conditioned jacket?

An attractive option enthusiastically favoured by some is to buy a well-tailored anorak of very close-woven cotton.

21

This is normally breathable, but in rain the cotton fibres expand to close gaps and the garment is then proof. But this too can be expensive.

Yet another choice is waxed cotton; waterproofing is usually effective but it needs re-waxing occasionally. The advantage of waxed cloth is that it is fairly stiff and hangs loosely enough to allow a certain amount of inner air circulation. But some do not like the feel of it against inner garments. Lined waxed jackets are available and are excellent in winter, but unbearably stuffy in summer. I find waxed cotton over-trousers too hot also. Separated 'leggings' covering the legs only to the thighs, as our shepherds often wear, are better; but they are designed to pull over large boots, and lacking zips they are like cowboys' chaps, too 'floppy' for walking comfortably.

Obviously the wearer of ordinary waterproofs will warm up. The only remedy is to reduce perspiration by slowing the pace. One uncomfortable hot region at the waist, where trousers and coat overlap, is not helped by elasticized waist-bands on the over-trousers. A solution that some find helpful is to do away with the elastic and fit braces instead.

Why bother about waterproofs? Pick the day and carry an umbrella? What I have said about clothing is not holy writ; everyone can wear what they like. The point is that country walkers are free when they are equipped for everything the climate can throw at them. Anyway, there is no harm in getting a *little* wet so long as the body is kept warm.

Clothing is a means to an end, and in this case the end is the freedom to enjoy the countryside without worrying about what the weatherman can bring.

You may think, by the way, that those Scottish drovers had got it right. Trust the crafty Scots to know how to deal with the weather's hardships. 90 square feet of woollen weave will do the trick? Apparently not. It was a Scotsman who rejected that idea and invented the first real waterproof – a Mr MacIntosh.

4

Equipment

What to carry? By comparison with the burden of worries left behind, very little. The object of a country walk is to get away from it all, not to bring it all with you. If the amount of enjoyment of the countryside is in direct proportion to the amount left behind, then one must travel very lightly.

First of all, for a full day's walk, you require a sack to contain your needs. A haversack is the traditional receptacle – a pity that word 'haversack' is being super-seded by the German word 'rucksack', the 'back sack'. A haversack – or 'havermeal poak', or 'havermeal pauk' in Scots and Cumbrian – has an ancient origin. It was the shoulder pouch which carried the 'haver' or oats, which as oatmeal was the staple diet for the drover of old – either baked as biscuits on a wayside fire, or mixed with water (in his shoe!) and eaten raw – a kind of crude muesli. My sack is often a haversack, for crisp Scottish oatcakes are my favourite food outdoors. They cannot be beaten – with a hunk of cheese and a Cox's Orange apple. Alas, gone are the days when Cumbrian 'haverbread' was readily available and variable as 'thick, thin, clap, riddle, girdle, squares or snaps' made in warm-hearthed farm kitchens by warm-hearted farm housewives.

So a 'rucksack' containing the necessary life support system is the answer, as it allows the arms and hands to be free. It is a mistake to acquire a sack of a thin material, no matter how strong. Not only will it take on the shape of the objects inside – and hard lumpy things like thermos flasks make painful impressions on the back – but the material itself can cling closely, trapping an area of perspiration. A stiffish canvas-like material is more suitable, and should be of more than ample capacity. In an inadequate one, the objects being too tightly packed shape the sack into a hard football and the thing will hang abominably. One good rucksack could serve for a family, but it is not a bad idea for families to share the burden. Children often prefer to carry their own things and there are child-size sacks available.

The rucksack carries the modest needs of the day: food and drink, waterproofs, spare sweater, a simple first-aid kit. Other necessaries best carried in the coat pockets are notebook and pencil, a map, and bird or flower identification books.

THE MAP
A map is the most important item of equipment, the key to the freedom of the outdoors. Once the simple reading technique is grasped and practised it becomes the ideal countryside companion – and sometimes a fireside friend on winter nights when a past adventure is re-lived or a future one planned. To an explorer every map means discovery, so choose maps with care and cherish them. They can give a lifetime of pleasure.

The minimum requirement, and the least expensive, would be a map to the scale of 1 inch to the mile. In Britain this is available for some tourist regions, published by the Ordnance Survey and by Bartholomew of Edinburgh. The larger scale Ordnance Survey maps have greater detail and are easy to use, but more than one map may be needed to cover the distance of a walk. There is the popular 1:50 000 series (2cm to 1km – approximately 1¼ inches to the mile).

In Ireland the Ordnance Survey produces 1-inch scale maps for the whole country, in black outline only; and the 1:50 000 are becoming available.

There are 1:25 000 maps in the United Kingdom covering some tourist regions (4cm to 1km, approximately 2½ inches to the mile). These give an enormous amount of detail, but cover a relatively small area. For instance you would need four of them to cover the central area of the Lake District National Park, and four for Snowdonia National Park. An admirable map of this scale published by the Manx Department of Highways, Ports and Properties covers the whole of the Isle of Man, however.

A map is of little use unless the owner is a skilled map-reader. Map-reading is dealt with in Chapter 5.

GUIDE BOOK

Take a walkers' guide book: there are many available nowadays – some excellent, some indifferent, and some poor. They should at least have a good map or plan of each walk. Most are designed to be carried on the walk but others, heavier and bulkier, are best consulted at home in the planning stage and left there. The advantage of a good guide book is that it suggests the best walks and the best features in the area. Without a local guide there is the possibility of missing the most important features. Another advantage, assuming that the book has been well-researched, is that there is less possibility of meeting with problems and obstructions. The disadvantage is that if used exclusively there is no need to practise map-reading and initiative is sapped.

A poor guide book can lead one into all kinds of difficulties – barbed wire, irate landowners, bogs, and rough hill walks unsuitable and sometimes dangerous to the average walker. Some are written by authors who only *think* that they know the area, and are unclear on what is and what is not a public right of way. One problem with all guide books is that they can soon be outdated: trees mentioned in the directions might be felled, fields are sometimes planted, fords (hopefully!) become bridges, stiles become gates or vice versa.

The problem is that too often one cannot judge a guide book's effectiveness from a cursory inspection in the bookshop. *Check that the author states that all the routes mentioned are public rights of way and established permissive routes, or on open land to which the public has access.* A great deal of trouble is caused to farmers and landowners – and to the walkers – by guide-book authors who have not researched the status of path or land. Look to see if the included maps and plans are clear, and check if the points of interest on the routes are highlighted and explained.

SUSTENANCE

In the rucksack carry food and drink. A bottled drink is a bad idea, glass is heavy. A thermos flask, or canned or cartoned drinks are fine. White wine will stay chilled in a thermos flask. Best to keep drink containers in a plastic bag in case of leakage (I can tell you that leaking carrot and parsnip soup makes a mess!). Sandwiches, or whatever, are best kept in plastic bags or boxes.

Walkers are usually advised to carry something for their meal containing sugar or glucose for instant energy. Just take whatever suits you: caviare, or steak-and-kidney pie if preferred. After all, the al fresco meal is a very vital part of the gentle art of country walking. Food can be pure ambrosia eaten in the open air.

The identification of a good place to eat, without undue delay in the finding, is a true mark of skill in the gentle art of country walking. The dining places should be remembered well. I have many happy memories – let me count a few: the shelter in a high lakeland cave, on a slashing rainy winter's day; a great viewpoint over a bustling Scottish harbour; an amazing awesome perch on the cliffs of Buchail Etive Mor in Glencoe, when the wind held breath; back leaning against the Inaccessible Pinnacle on a misty Isle of Skye; by a waterfall overhung by rowan berries where Wordsworth once walked; out of a hostile wind in a perfectly fitting rock hollow on Snowdon; leaning on a sun-baked wall of a Spanish castle high above the Mediterranean; sitting on a massive fallen trunk in an American rain forest with light filtering through the great high trees; in a Dartmoor fog, watched by some mysterious ancient stones; in sunshine by an Exmoor beacon, while the sea far below was hidden in mist and only distant foghorns occasionally broke utter silence; in a flower-filled meadow with the scent of thyme, atop the white cliffs of Dover; and another heavy with a medley of scents high in the Julian alps; lounging amongst heather in warm November sunshine on the Isle of Man; sharing a bench by an Irish cottage door (sampling my first nip of potheen); in a favourite spot loud with bird-song by a woodland pool. I add to them every year. Yes, take whatever you feel is right, and find your own dining-room! There are millions of them all finely furnished for your convenience. *Bon appetit!*

Not a good idea to overload the stomach, though. The walk has to go on!

It is also a good idea to have some energy-giving sweets – or better, dried fruit – tucked away as morale-boosting 'iron rations' in case a delayed journey lengthens an agonizing time between meal breaks.

Don't forget to put a plastic bag in the sack to take the meal litter back home; cans can easily be squashed to take up less room. A true country walker with a care for the countryside also picks up any other trash left by ignorant louts who should know better.

FIRST-AID KIT

Find room in the sack for a small first-aid kit. No need to take enough to deal with a major disaster: a plastic box containing an assortment of plaster dressings for minor cuts or blisters, an elastic bandage, paper tissues, a wound-dressing, a tube of whatever the chemist recommends for insect stings and bites, a small pair of scissors, safety-pins, aspirin. In the same box one could pack insect repellent, and a needle and thread for emergency clothing repairs. (*See* Appendix 3.)

SUNDRIES

What else? Anything that might be useful and is of little weight. I carry a small 10x magnifying glass for looking at tiny things; a favourite sharp penknife (which I seem to have often used for cutting sheep out from tangled brambles!); book matches; coins in a place aside in case I need to use a telephone box; a length of strong tape for tying, securing, or lowering things (I do not know quite what, but I would feel lost without it!); an Army issue tin and bottle opener, and corkscrew. Like all hill-walkers I carry a whistle, handy if I wish to attract attention should I have an immobilizing accident, for more often than not I walk alone. I have the whistle on my rucksack cord, which incidentally could serve to replace a broken bootlace.

In high summer, if walking in wet areas or forests, that fly repellent is a necessity! Midges, particularly the Scottish Highland sort, can drive strong men mad. A fortunate minority of folk are practically immune to bites, but others will need the potent protective stuff developed for use in the world's jungles. Sun specs and some sun lotion to prevent burning might be added.

In earlier days no walker's equipment was complete without a sketch-pad. Nowadays many will feel the need to carry a 35mm camera to record those scenes and magical moments. There are lightweights and compacts, but I favour a heavier metal veteran which withstands, as I learned, a bounce on a rocky floor, and happens to have some good lenses. Scenic shots come out best on slower film; but on cloudy days one may wish for something faster; and faster films – 200 ASA and above – are nowadays much better than they once were.

Binoculars are needed for bird-watchers. Modern ones are by no means as heavy and bulky as they used to be. 'Roof prism' types can be slipped into a pocket. Around 8 × 30 are ideal, as they view a wide field.

'THIRD LEG'

A walking-stick? Yes, if one is needed, but it does mean that only one hand is free. I was grateful to be given one when I was handicapped by a damaged knee, and I sometimes use it on low-level walks in snow and ice. Some people would not be without a stick, and it becomes a constant companion. A stick is also useful for pointing out landmarks to the less knowledgeable of the walker's party, acting as a steadying 'monopod' in taking photographs, hooking down out-of-reach bramble berries, and fending off hungry children with unreasonable designs on the iron rations!

A longer, stout thumb stick is an asset – some would say vital – in rough moorland to aid a jump over a water-course. And fording a fast-flowing stream can be very hazardous without a longish steadying 'third leg'. In off-the-path walking, it is also useful for testing the firmness of doubtful ground ahead.

Years ago when working in a forest, my spare-time hobby was cutting and shaping sticks. The first task was to seek a straight shaft of suitable wood amongst the coppice. Hazel was the easiest to find, since it sends out so many shoots from its coppice 'stool' (the rooted stump). Some grow as straight as billiard cues, and with suitable forks at the right height presented ready-made thumb sticks. Harder to find was a shoot growing up from a horizontal stem or root, to make a walking-stick with a natural crook. Hazels make admirable sticks. Ash also grows straight stems from the coppice stools quickly, and these make very reliable sticks too; they are probably the most common on sale. Hawthorn, blackthorn, holly or yew are harder to find, but I think make the best sticks of all. Most other woods can be rejected as being too brittle or too heavy. If a stick must be had, choose a strong one with a straight grain. Avoid painted or heavily varnished sticks, since the wood is disguised by this treatment and flaws can be obscured. To be the correct length a walking-stick should touch ground with the fore-arm bent just lower than horizontal; a thumb stick at breastbone height. Sticks should have a metal tip, or ferrule; it is possible to slip a rubber one over this when walking on paving.

CASH

Any money needed, real or plastic, should be carried on the person, not in the sack. Money? Who needs money on a country walk? None for a glass of cool cider in that little village pub on the way? And many who are disgracefully decadent think that a good walk is made even better when it finishes at a wayside café with a cream tea with fresh scones and home-made jam! Some gifted walkers can find such places by instinct . . .

5

Basic Map-Reading

What is astonishing about history, when one considers, is how the Romans could march out and conquer the huge area of Europe, north beyond the Black Sea and the Danube, and west to half the British Isles; the Middle East and North Africa with all their complicated physical structures of mountains, forests, river valleys, estuaries and plains – all *without maps*.

Nearer the present times, one can marvel at the way the pioneers of the American continent explored vast regions and returned to tell the tale.

Until only two centuries ago, land maps which did exist were usually woefully inaccurate. Land travel even throughout the more or less civilized areas of the British Isles and Europe, and maybe only short distances, was largely by guesswork and 'askwork'.

With the added hazards of ill-maintained ways, and the likelihood of robbery, a journey was a serious undertaking. To reach one's destination without going astray was an accomplishment; those venturing were advised to first put their affairs in order, and on the journey to make serious use of the wayside chapels.

One of the classic adventures was to wander into untrodden and unmapped territory. Little chance now, for with only a few limitations it is possible to make maps from the air.

If we wander too far from familiar surroundings and do not want to go astray we need a map: that much scaled-down, two-dimensional crow's-eye picture of the land-scape. A map is an invitation to the countryside, the key to adventure.

UNDERSTANDING

But we cannot take our map-*reading* for granted. Every walker soon learns that map-reading for a walk is not as simple as navigating the main highways in a vehicle. Roads are obvious to the eye and more often than not are lavishly signposted. Public footpaths are often hard to see and although highway authorities in England and Wales are obliged by law to signpost them at the point where they leave a road, signposts are disgracefully scarce in many regions. Having reached open country either there may be no paths visible at all, or misleading paths going every which-way. Good map-reading is vital to a day's enjoyment.

Having acquired a map, the first thing is to understand the map-makers' symbols and letters. Somewhere on the side of the map these are explained. For instance, there may be symbols or letters for churches, telephone kiosks, sites of antiquity, public houses and, on larger-scale maps, viewpoints, information centres and car parks.

Basic map-reading is very simple after a little practice. Commencing a walk and (presumably) knowing where your starting point is on the map, the first task is to orientate. Literally this is determining the direction of east; but north is always at the top of the map, and the map-reader had best turn around until the top of the map is interfaced with actual north. There are two ways of doing this. First, there is orientation by landmarks. For instance, if reading the map indicates that there is a church to the westward of the starting point, it is only necessary to hold the map the right way up and turn yourself round until the church observed is on the left, and in line with the church symbol on the map. The top of the map is then aligned to north; and it is possible to identify other physical details in their respective places, and the position of the required footpath.

The second way, particularly if there are no obvious landmarks to assist, is to use a pocket compass. Most compasses come with (a) a rim marked with the cardinal points, the north point shown prominently and accentuated by marked parallel lines in the compass bowl base, and (b) the magic magnetic needle, its northern end painted red (fig. 1). The compass is placed on the map (away from steel; this does not work on the top of a car bonnet!) with the north pointer of the compass *rim and bowl base* lining up with the top of the map. This is easier if there are vertical grid lines on the map, and vertical lines on the transparent compass bowl, for the two can then be aligned in parallel. With the compass held firmly in place on the map, turn yourself around while watching the compass needle's red end until it comes into line with the north point on the compass rim and bowl base.

You and the map are then roughly orientated; but not quite, for the compass needle points to *magnetic* north, not true north. So you, the map and compass together must be turned slightly to the right until the compass needle points to around 6 degrees to the west (left) of the north line: 354 degrees (this in 1992 in Britain, for the magnetic north annoyingly changes very slowly over the years and from region to region, all of which should be explained on the side or base of the map). You and the map are then correctly orientated.

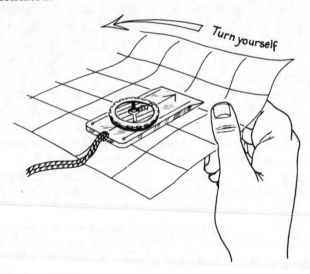

fig. 1 – Orienting yourself to the map

stage 1

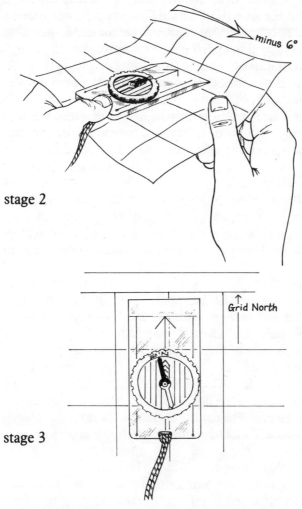

minus 6°

stage 2

Grid North

stage 3

If, like me, you have great mental difficulties in following instructions, even when written in good English, you may need to read and experiment with the foregoing again. (The finer details of the use of the compass are dealt with in the next chapter.)

Having orientated, the walker can then identify his line of travel. It comes easier after practice. As the walk proceeds the position on the map can be fixed by identifying landmarks, and by time checks. At a fairly average pace some 3 miles is covered in an hour, but the reckoning has to be adjusted to take account of stop times for admiring views or features, adjusting speed to slow members of the party, or photographing, or going over rough or rising ground.

After a deal of experience map-reading becomes second nature. Everyone, including the cleverest, makes mistakes from time to time; but it is a great source of satisfaction to find that calculations have worked out right in the end without the exercise spoiling the enjoyment of the walk.

MAP REFERENCES

It is possible to identify a precise point on an Ordnance Survey map by using a six-figure map reference. You may not need to do this very often, but it is as well to know how to go about it. The way it works is explained on the map margin.

The map is ruled out in a grid of kilometre squares. To fix a reference one must first make note of the two-digit number reference of the vertical grid line to the left (west) of the locality; this gives the first two figures. Then imagine the square in which the locality lies is divided into ten vertical lines. Estimate on which division east of the vertical grid line the locality lies and note that number (the third reference number) (*see* fig. 2). Next note the two-figure number of the grid line south, *below* the locality (the fourth and fifth numbers). Lastly, imagine that the square again is divided into ten *horizontal* lines upwards and note the number of that imaginary line (there is the six-figure reference). The most common mistake in working out references is to work from the horizontal grid line first instead of the vertical. (I once read about a Roman Fort site at 'map reference 378038', which could put it somewhere off the north coast of the Isle of Man. It should have read 038378.)

Properly, the six-figure number should be prefixed with

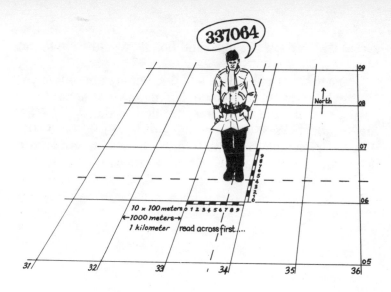

fig. 2 – Explaining grid references

the two letters which identify the map. These are shown on the OS map margin where the map references are explained.

The Irish OS maps also carry grid lines, but the system is slightly different. A reference has a letter followed by six figures. Each square has a letter which must be noted. For the three figures right (east) of the vertical grid line of the square one must give a two-figure distance in kilometres followed by a single figure for the additional hectometre (tenth of a kilometre). A similar note is made upwards from the horizontal.

A minor warning – maps are not always exactly up to date. You may find a new building that is not shown, newly planted woodland or – rarely – an actual mistake by the cartographer. In the course of a walk I once found a large area of old woodland in the remote Scottish Highlands apparently undiscovered by the OS map-maker. Maybe the map-maker was confused by a persistent Scots' mist and left the area blank? In ancient times he would have written across it, 'Here be dragons' and no one would have found him out . . .

Come to think of it, Highland dragons are not unknown. Once while staying at a remote Highland guest house I was poring over my map, making ambitious walking plans for the Sunday. 'You'll be going to the kirk,' said the proprietary female dragon. I am no hero. I modified my intentions, I put away the map, I went to the kirk.

6

The Art of Navigation
and the Compass

Why do human beings have difficulty in finding their way around when the lowliest of creatures manage quite well? To return home from unfamiliar territory only a matter of a few miles from home, we have to resort to reading signposts and maps. We have always known that birds do rather better: the ancient Egyptians were using homing pigeons to carry messages four thousand years ago. The Arctic tern can nest in the Arctic Circle, migrate right across the globe to the Antarctic, at least 11,000 miles away, and return 11,000 miles again unerringly and absolutely accurately to its own nesting site. Ronald Lockley, who lived for thirteen years on an island off the Pembrokeshire coast and established Britain's first bird observatory, had two of the island's shearwaters carried by air to be released in Venice 930 miles away. Although the Mediterranean was completely unknown to shearwaters, one of them returned home, well-fed, within fourteen days. The other arrived the following spring. How could this be possible?

Many experiments have been made which seem to prove that bird, and even insect, migrants navigate by the sun by day and the stars by night. Even when the sun is obscured by cloud its position can be detected by the acute senses of birds. We know that if incoming diffused light is polarized with filters it is possible to fix the light source, and it is assumed that migrating species have this facility. But fixing the position of the sun by day, or the constellations by night, is not enough. As the earth constantly turns on its axis the sun is only due south in the northern hemisphere, and due north in the southern hemisphere, at noon. Nature's navigators have to have a built-in clock so that they will know what the sun's position should be at any given time. It has long been known that even the most minuscule forms of life have this time sense built into their genes, which defy scientific attempts to fool it.

But to fix direction is not enough. A migrating bird, having found out which way, must know how far. It must fix its position relative to the equator, and to do this it must be aware of the angle with which the light of the sun reaches it, and must relate that to a built-in calendar!

This seems incredible, since to determine the position of a ship at sea we have long had to rely on an accurate chronometer, an almanac, and a precision instrument – the sextant – to measure the sun's angle.

There is still a tremendous amount to learn from nature's travellers; we are only on the outermost fringe of such knowledge. We know that as well as the inbuilt navigating sense, animals and birds have acute memory for every detail of place. Domestic cats and dogs, taken miles from home into strange territory, can find the way home. Some have made incredible journeys. There is much that is incomprehensible. The limpet, for instance, creeps along its rock, grazing on algae when the tide is out. When the tide comes in it returns precisely to its own special place, even when scientists have covered its eyes and altered the shape of the rock around with chisel and acid. Scent plays its part – amazingly in the case of salmon which, it is thought, find their way with their olfactory organs from the vast open sea to their own river, and then on up to the spawning beds where they were born. But more, we know that nature has its own radar system, that a bird or a bat can land precisely where it wants to do in the dark by emitting a cry and measuring the echo.

How much, if any, is left to us of that basic instinct of navigation? We all experience the 'pull' of the safety and warmth of home, and if away from our original home for a time we can feel 'nostalgic'. Is this the remnant of something deep down, in the subconscious twilight? And we still have a sense of time to a lesser or a greater degree, even though we need to rely on the accuracy of mechanical or electronic aid. If we are accustomed to rising at 7 a.m. seven days each week, it should become unnecessary to employ an alarm clock: our body knows when to wake up. If we have doubts about an inner clock, we can be made uncomfortably aware that it exists after a long journey when we suffer from jet-lag.

Before the discovery of the magnetic compass the mariners of ancient times seemed to move around reasonably well. Memory would have played a great part as they hugged the coasts, and knowledge of the tides and seasons which was passed down through generations. The changing position of the stars and planets, and the phases of the moon, were keenly known to all from pre-history. Note the alignments of the ancient stone circles, for example. As far back as the early traders, such as the Phoenicians, navigators must have used such knowledge to determine their position at night.

But the sextant and the compass were needed to discover the continents over shifting currents and winds above the vast oceans.

Some of us boast that we have 'a good sense of direction'. How many are like me? I am never happy in strange territory – even in the middle of a city (cities are the worst) – until I have worked out the direction of north! I can usually do it after a glance at the sun if it is visible, and at my watch; though a good look at a map beforehand helps! But there was one occasion – I was in the middle of Birmingham – when I had to jump out of my car and look at my compass to determine in which direction I had to turn to get to the motorway. Although I have made several visits to the beautiful city of Bath, I have always had difficulty in finding my way back from the outside to the centre. Planned cities are the catch, for the 'grid' system of streets keeps one on rigid lines. No matter where I am, long experience has taught me to be cautious in relying too much on my sense of direction.

Some hill-walkers tell me that they have managed to walk for years without a compass. All I can say is that they have been fortunate in being able to choose clear daylight weather for their excursions. It is possible to enjoy years of low-level walking without a compass, but a compass makes it all so easy. For ordinary low-level walking we can use it to orientate occasionally, or to determine direction. If a walker is to make for the open country of hills and moorland he should know and practice the finer skills. It is actually quite fun.

Yes, we all make idiotic mistakes. Several times, in silly situations on the fells, my compass has saved me from embarrassment.

What must be remembered is that no one can walk naturally in a straight line. Left to itself, the walking process takes the walker in a curve, because the stride of one leg is slightly longer than that of the other. This becomes patently obvious from experiment. A blindfolded person might be convinced that he is walking directly to an objective, but he seldom makes it. The longer the distance, the greater the error.

The earth is in effect a huge magnet, but the magnetic field changes very slightly during each day; and over years it moves slightly eastwards and westwards. A magnetic needle pivoted on a horizontal plane will constantly align itself north and south with the magnetic, not the geographical, poles.

USING A COMPASS

So how to use a compass to work out and walk on a bearing in open country? The following advice need not be studied if you intend to keep to low-level footpaths and do not wish to go into the finer details of compass work. However, every walker should have a compass and some may feel that they want their money's worth out of it.

First, to repeat the warning about using the compass near to steel or magnets. If you have a camera, or a separate light meter for it, keep them well away! Otherwise heaven knows where your wayward walk will take you. There are places in the mountains where a strong magnetic field in the earth deflects compass needles; but these are rare, and do not necessarily have any effect unless the compass is placed on the ground.

As stated earlier, the best type of compass is set in a

transparent bowl fixed into a transparent oblong plate. Looking at the OS map we see that it is drawn out in that grid of squares. The verticals run north and south, or nearly so; it cannot be absolutely accurate as the earth is curved and the map is flat. The diagram on the side of the map showing the north points might show three: true, grid, and magnetic. But the first two are so near to each other that we can ignore the difference.

Now, supposing that in open country without known landmarks we reach a point on the map which shows one path, but on the ground there are three. Which is the right one? It can be determined quickly with the use of the compass. Place the side of the compass base alongside the correct path shown on the map, with the arrow on the base thus pointing in the required direction of travel. Ignoring the needle, hold the compass base in position while turning

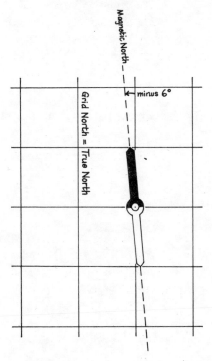

fig. 3 – Grid/Magnetic and true north

41

the compass bowl until the vertical lines in its transparency line up with the map's vertical grid lines, with the bowl's north mark at the top. The bearing figure can then be read off at the point touched by the direction of travel line in the base (*see* fig. 4). The bearing can be taken as aligned to true north, and it is now necessary to convert it to magnetic north simply by adding 6 degrees.

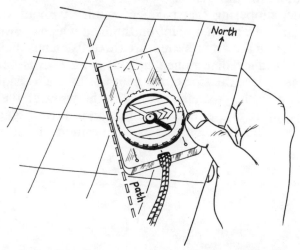

fig. 4 – Selecting the correct path – from map to ground stage 1

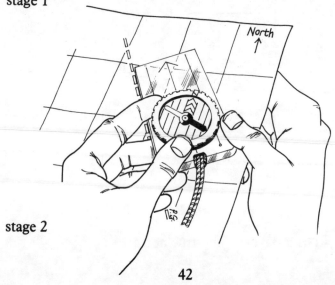

stage 2

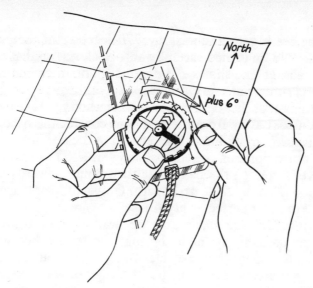

North

plus 6°

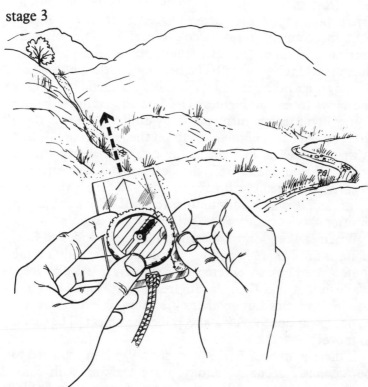

If the bearing reading was, say, 270 degrees, the compass bowl should be turned carefully anti-clockwise so that the travel marker line shows 276 degrees. (The marks on the compass rim are at every 2 degrees.)

Holding it at that figure, it is now necessary to take eyes and compass away from the map and consult the needle. Turn *yourself* around until the red end of the needle points to the north point on the compass bowl rim. The direction of travel arrow on the base plate then points towards the direction taken by the correct path. Only a little practice is needed to get it perfect every time.

Having done the above exercise, walking on a bearing becomes possible. It might be that the terrain becomes pathless in open country. Having worked out exactly where you are on the map, lay the edge of the compass plate from that starting point to the next objective, with its arrow pointing in the correct direction of travel. Again, turn the compass bowl to co-ordinate its lines with the vertical grid lines. (Always remember to keep the bowl's north marking upwards!) The bearing can then be read off as above, and the reading changed to magnetic by turning the bowl to *add* 6 degrees. Holding the compass before you, you must then turn your body until the red end of the magnetic needle points to north on the bowl rim. All that is then needed is to walk in the direction shown by the arrow. If you wander off the bearing you will know at once, as the needle will have swung away from the north point, and it is necessary to turn yourself until it is back in position.

When walking on the bearing, it is a good idea to look along it until there is an identifiable object exactly on the route – perhaps an outcrop of rock or a particular tree. Walk to that and then, having reached it, look along the bearing and pick out another object and walk to that, and so on. (Best not to pick a sheep for the object. They tend to move!)

If there is an occasion in open country when you need to be *absolutely* accurate, and you are walking with companions, it is easy to walk at the rear, put them in single file,

44

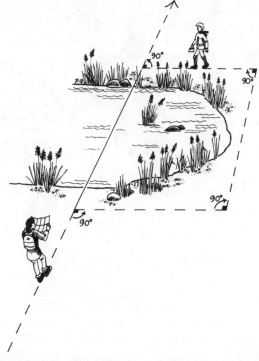

fig. 5 – Negotiating obstacles in your path

and direct them along the right line.

Should a detour be necessary, say to get around a bog, turn 90 degrees, count the paces necessary to get by, then again turn 90 degrees until the far side of the bog is reached; turn 90 degrees once more and count the paces to get back on to the correct line, then turn 90 degrees again to follow the bearing *see* (fig. 5).

If the walk on a bearing to an unseen objective is a longish one, it is unlikely that it will be reached absolutely 'spot-on'. No matter how accurately a walker may tread his bearing, there is likely to be some undetected sideways movement. You could still be walking on the bearing, but on a line parallel to the original one. Sometimes the objective might be a gateway in a wall, and having reached the barrier and not found the gateway it is guesswork as to

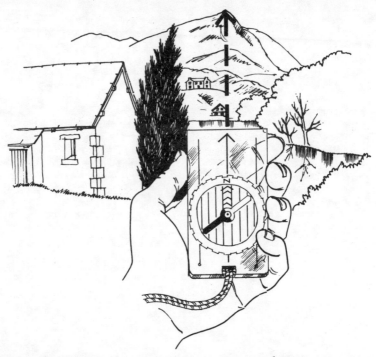

fig. 6 – Locating a feature using compass and map

whether one seeks it to the right or to the left. One trick used by orienteers is to *deliberately* aim the bearing to the left of the objective; then, having reached the wall, it is known that the gateway should be to the right.

BEARINGS TO LANDMARKS

A bearing can be taken from a viewpoint to identify landmarks, or to fix position. In these cases the above operation is taken in reverse. To identify a landmark from a known position, point the direction-of-travel arrow on the base plate to it. Holding the plate in that position, carefully turn the compass bowl until the red end of the compass needle is aligned with the bowl's north point. The reading then taken at the direction-of-travel marker line will be the *magnetic* bearing. Before consulting the map it is necessary to correct it to true by *subtracting* 6 degrees (turning the

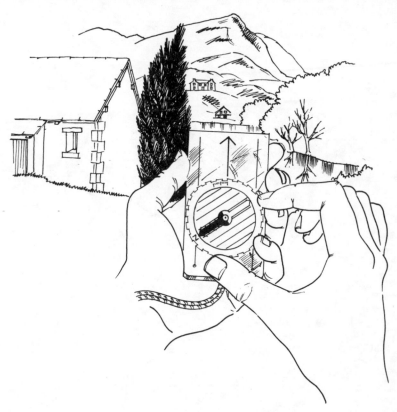

stage 2

compass bowl clockwise). Forgetting the needle, and placing the lower corner of the base plate on the map at the viewing point, turn the *map* until the lines in the compass bowl align themselves with the vertical grid lines. A pencil line can then be drawn along the edge of the base plate from the viewing point, and it will pass through the landmark to be identified (*see* fig.6).

If a similar procedure is used to fix one's position it is necessary to do so from *two recognizable* landmarks, preferably not close together – say two peaks. Use the same exercise as above; the bearing having been read, lay the compass on the map with its top corner at the first

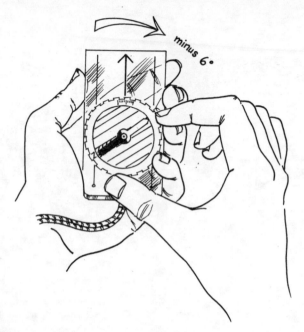

minus 6°

stage 3

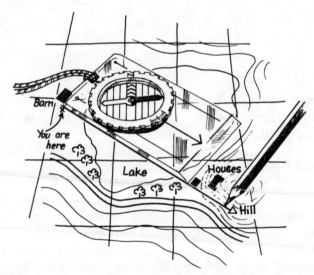

Barn

You are here

Lake

Houses

△ Hill

stage 4

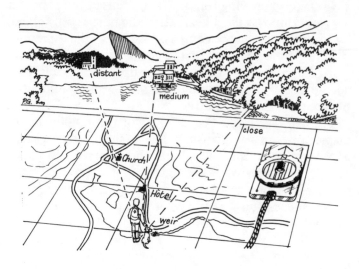

fig. 7 – Fixing your position from landmarks

landmark. If the map is then turned carefully so that the vertical lines in the compass bowl line up with the vertical grid lines, a pencil line can then be drawn along the base plate edge. Repeat the process on the second landmark and where the pencil lines cross is near enough to your position. It is unlikely to be absolutely accurate (to be so, one would need to use a prismatic compass). If wished, a line could be taken from a third landmark and the position might then be within a triangle of lines (*see* fig.7).

Some amusement in practice with the compass, possibly near home before setting out, could make its use second nature. To practice walking on a bearing, try hiding a pound coin in some grass, then pacing off on any bearing. Turn right 90 degrees for the same number of paces, add 90 degrees again for the same number of paces, and again, and the coin should be found. Lengthen the walk once confidence is gained.

One important point; if the compass is as handy as it should be on the open heights, it can be used to good advantage when a fog rolls in. If you can see the approach of fog (low cloud), take a bearing on the next visible objective by squinting along the compass base along the direction-of-travel arrow, and lining up the needle with the bowl's north mark *before* the way becomes obscured. Checking that the needle does not stray, you can then walk confidently on through the thickest murk.

The compass is to be used – not worn around the neck as a magic talisman – and trusted. There have been times when I have sworn that mine was lying and I have given it a good shaking. I have always apologized to it afterwards!

So, using our sophisticated equipment, we have navigated successfully. But what about the compass-less shepherd who is out in the hills in all weathers? Even though he might have lived in the area all his life, surely in bad conditions he must get lost occasionally? When I put this to one of my local shepherds whom I met in a hill fog, he pushed back his cap and scratched his head. 'Get lost? Nay!' And then he thought for a while and admitted that, yes, 'Yance (once) or twice.' Then what did he do? He smiled at me as if I was asking a daft question. 'Well then – I just followed m' dog!'

7

Planning

Someone said that to travel hopefully is a better thing than to arrive. Wherever one goes, hope is less likely to evaporate if the travel is planned with a little care. This means first sitting down with a map, working out the route on the public footpaths, and/or studying a good guide book for the locality.

The object of a country walk is to have a leisurely excursion, so enthusiasm for mileage should be curbed. After some experience the ideal distance to fit individual and group needs will be found. A family walk particularly must be planned with the weakest member in mind, though it is usual to underestimate a child's stamina. When children complain about being 'tired' on a walk, it often means that they are bored by the repetitive activity of moving legs and feet. A rest stop might find them running wildly around or playing football.

It is best if the walk has a variety of interesting features on the route; though things like baby ducklings, birds' nests, banks of flowers, viewpoints and human encounters are not marked on the map. To taste surprise is the essence of adventure. Surprise is the great gift that country walking can always offer.

Ideally, there might be a key objective on the route such as a ruined castle, an ancient monument, or a church, a waterfall, a picturesque village, an acclaimed viewpoint. Some detailed research on these points beforehand can be useful.

Plan to do about 3 miles per hour (5km); rather less, say 2½ miles per hour (4km), if the way is rough and hilly. Add a generous time allowance for stops, eating, staring at things, taking photographs; and then a bit for any unexpected hazards like blisters, shaky route finding, necessary route diversions, or the onset of blissful idleness. If there is some hill climbing on the route, check the contours and add an extra twenty minutes for every 500 feet (150m) of ascent.

Timing of course is vital if there is public transport to catch at the walk's end. Make sure that you have the timetable right, though. I once had to finish a highland walk at a long and weary 3-mile gallop, racing triumphantly to the village bus-stop just on time – only to find that the one and only bus did not run on Thursdays!

If public transport is available, the planned route can be from 'A to B'. Alas, public transport is a thing of the past in many rural parts following budget restrictions, withdrawal of subsidies and the run-down of the railways. The loss can have a devastating effect on some communities, though at least in some tourist areas a few summer services survive. Where only private transport can be used, the route planned has to be to and from it: from 'A to A'. To do this without having to route too much of the walk on public roads requires fine map-reading skill.

Having planned the route, some find it useful to note features on the map at the key points – where a path deviates from another for instance. The key points might look straightforward on the map, but on the ground there could be some obscurity. It helps if you know, for example, that at a key left turn there should be the corner of a wood to the right, and a group of buildings in forward distance.

The best plan is to organize the gear and the food the evening before the walk. Then get the weather forecast; local weather forecasts can be obtained by telephoning the number listed in the phone directory. Do not be easily put off. 'Showers and bright intervals' can often mean lots of sunshine and an occasional splash; it can also indicate the condition which makes the views reveal their best in colour, light and shade – what the photographer and the connoisseur of the country scene needs.

Naturally it can also mean the reverse, but be bold! As has been said, even the wet day offers its rewards, not least in healthy exercise; and whatever the weather it could seem great in retrospect, when enjoying the pure bliss of soaking stretched muscles in a hot bath.

PUBLIC RIGHTS OF WAY

It is vital to plan a walk so as to use the public rights of way wherever these can be identified. Public rights of way confer the right of passage on foot; in some cases by bicycle or on horseback. These rights may date back for centuries. They may be parts of Roman roads which themselves might have been 'improvements' on prehistoric Iron Age tracks – which before then could even have been hunters' routes following animal pathways in the ancient forest. Animals choose the easiest ways in rough terrain. Some may be pilgrimage routes, or ancient pack-horse paths or drove roads. Around villages they link scattered settlements to important places like the church, the shops, or the pub. Or they could be 'coffin roads' where of old the dead were carried, often for long distances, for burial in consecrated ground.

The ancient rights are as valid as those for public roads; but of course, to a highway authority, the needs of pedestrians have become far less important than those of the all-important motor vehicles, and one cannot expect high standards of footpath maintenance, though sometimes it is possible to be delightfully surprised. However, not only would it be foolish to expect all public footpaths in the countryside to be paved; it would also be very undesirable – an objectionable urbanizing. One should be able to expect them to be unobstructed and reasonably drained, and signed or waymarked where necessary, though generally this is less likely.

There are approximately 135,000 miles (217,000 kms) of public rights of way in England and Wales, and they can be identified on up-to-date maps with a reference to the symbol keys on the map's border. On some maps the routes are marked in green (which is unfortunate when they pass through green-coloured woods). The OS 1:50 000 series, and the 1 inch to the mile mark them in red. Dotted lines represent public footpaths, dashed lines public bridleways (the *only* rights of way usable by cyclists and horse-riders).

'Permissive paths' – that is those that are not rights of way, but whose use is permitted by the landowner – are difficult to identify. They are usually shown as black dots or dashes, and there is no way of distinguishing them from private routes which are also shown. However, the new 1:25 000 OS maps are beginning to show permissive paths as brown dots. Permissive paths are more often than not signed.

It is sometimes also difficult to distinguish between private roads and unmetalled *highways*, the 'green roads' or '*byways*'. If an unmetalled track joins on to public rights of way, it will almost certainly be a byway – that is a road which can be used by pedestrians, horse-riders, cyclists and vehicle drivers (the latter at their own risk). Some maps show the byways with a symbol marked 'road used as public path', others as 'byways open to traffic'.

Assuming that most of the walking is done not far from home and that a map has not been previously studied, you may be surprised how many public rights of way there are in the area. If the route is planned to use them, the walk can be taken happily in the knowledge that progress is within the law and no landowner can properly challenge one with trespass. Here I should try to explain the law.

USERS

A public right of way in England and Wales confers a right of passage on foot on footpaths; and on foot, horseback or bicycle on bridleways. No one, not even the owner of the land over which the path runs, has the right to interfere with passage. The landowner cannot argue that the path is wrongly marked on the map. After past legal process and local consultations in the drafting, required by the National Parks and Access to the Countryside Act of 1949, the rights of way are shown on a definitive map held by the highway authority (usually the County Council) and on view at local government offices. Once on this map, their establishment has the force of law. The rights of way shown on the OS and Bartholomew's 1 inch to the mile and larger-scale maps are copied from the definitive map. There is a possibility of

54

some mistakes, but these are unusual; though sometimes maps can be out of date. A landowner can seek to alter the line of a path or bridleway through a legal process; if the line has been legally altered, the new route should be sign-posted.

Right of passage on a public right of way means just that: a walker is legally entitled to walk the way. He has no right to stop on the path for longer than a short rest, no right to stop for an over-long picnic or a bathe in a stream, or to stay in one place for a long time – for instance for bird-watching. Most landowners are reasonable about this, but I had a family complain to me that they had to abandon a path-side sunbathe when a gamekeeper ordered them to move on. I had to explain that the agent of the landowner was within his rights. Such situations are rare, however. What quite rightly annoys landowners is when liberties are taken too far; for instance, when dogs are left to run loose, fires lit, picnic debris left behind, watercourses dammed by stones, gates that should be closed left open, and so on.

OBSTRUCTIONS
I wish I could say that it would be unusual to come across an obstructed footpath. In some counties the position is very bad, and their highway authorities – which have responsibility for the maintenance of rights of way, and law enforcement – are either dilatory at best, or non-cooperative at worst. A survey by the Countryside Commission in 1989 showed that 18 per cent of the footpath network in England and Wales was obstructed by plough-ing, was overgrown, fenced or walled up. Conditions varied very much between counties, but on average the Commission reckoned that walkers setting out on a walk of 2 miles stood a two-in-three chance of running into obstacles of some kind. And this more than forty years after the law required highway authorities to define and maintain them! It is a sad indictment of the lethargic local government system. In 1991 the Commission hoped for central government and local authority support to bring the whole of the rights of way network into good order by the year 2000;

surely an inordinately long time to catch up on what should have been done in the 1950s and 1960s.

One argument against the continuance of a right of way – that the fact that it is overgrown proves it is no longer used – is specious. It is more likely that it is unused because it has long been impassable.

No obstruction should go unreported and the precise location (ideally with a map reference) and the type of obstruction should be detailed. If highway authorities fail to respond to complaints within a reasonable time, the matter should be taken further. Advice and support can be obtained from the Ramblers Association; indeed, any walker who feels strongly about obstructed paths should consider membership of this Association.

I find it difficult to be sympathetic to a landowner who knowingly and deliberately obstructs a right of way. It may be an embarrassment to him; it may interfere with the efficient commercial use of his land; but he has the opportunity in law to apply for diversions, when successful compromises on the line of the route can be reached.

Should a walker come upon an obstruction he has the right to remove it sufficiently to allow passage for him and his party. If the party is reasonably agile, any such removal should be minimal. If the walker has grandma in the party, who might be (though not always nowadays!) less agile, he obviously has the right to remove the obstruction drastically.

A walker has no right to go deliberately to remove a known obstruction from a right of way; he can only legally remove it if he happens upon it in the course of the walk. The removal of a *known* obstruction is the responsibility of the highway authority, who may order the landowner to remove it; or if he refuses, can remove it and charge him for the expense of doing so.

A farmer can properly plough through a public right of way if it crosses arable land, subject to conditions. He can apply to the highway authority for a temporary diversion, which if agreed should be signposted. Otherwise, under the Rights of Way Act of 1990 a farmer who ploughs through a right of way must make the line of the path apparent and clear on the ground within fourteen days and keep it clear of growing crops. If the path is not cleared, the new Act gives the local authority the right to give twenty-four hours notice, and then move on to the land to clear the path and charge the farmer for the cost. Any path at the edge of a field must be left free.

A walker may properly deviate a reasonable distance from a right of way if it is obstructed say by deep mud, or if it has been undermined by a stream or the sea, or if it is flooded.

With the exception of bicycles on bridleways, no vehicle may be driven along a public footpath or bridleway. However, the landowner and his agents could have right of access for vehicles along the way to their property. A cyclist on a bridleway must give way to walkers.

The landowner cannot legally erect a sign on a path which might discourage or mislead walkers: for instance 'Private Road' signs, which in theory would be quite correct if the landowner was intending the sign to prohibit vehicle drivers. But the sign might imply to an uncertain map-reader that there was no way for walkers. The sign should also say 'Public Footpath' or 'Public Footpath Only'; or there should be a separate footpath sign nearby. I know of one landowner who wrote 'Public Footpath' on a 'Private' sign so small (and very neatly!) that one needed a magnifying-glass to read it. However, he did not get away with it. There are other illegal signs calculated to discourage walkers. What about 'Beware of Adders' – a choice one. One landowner I know went even better and added below this 'Nearest Serum . . .', quoting a hospital some thirty miles away. Even where adders are common, the likelihood of them lurking on footpaths to waylay walkers is in the realm of fantasy fiction. At the approach of humans, adders retreat scared very rapidly. Living for many years in an area where adders are very common, the only bites I have heard of have been received by incredibly foolish people who have caught the snakes and picked them up.

The highway authorities in England and Wales are

required in law to erect a 'footpath' sign at the point where public rights of way leave a public road. However, the 1949 Act did not specify a time limit and in many counties the signposting programme is of disgracefully low priority. Signposting varies tremendously over the country. Some authorities have set splendid examples, and there has been very noticeable progress in the National Parks, the designated Country Parks, and Areas of Outstanding Natural Beauty. But one cannot rely on finding a sign to confirm one's map-reading skill.

A highway authority or a voluntary organization acting on its behalf – such as a rambling club – can also waymark along routes where there might otherwise be confusion. This is normally done with yellow markers for footpaths and blue for bridleways. Waymarking generally is not all that common, and is not all that effective if it is not maintained afterwards. However, sometimes the waymarking keeps people on the line of the path so that after a time it becomes visible on the ground and waymark maintenance is no longer necessary.

If a footpath shown on a map is not indicated as a right of way, it does not necessarily mean that the public cannot use it. It may not have been claimed. The landowner may not object to people using it; he may allow its permissive use, in which case it should be appropriately signposted.

On the Isle of Man (which by the way offers some excellent walking for families as well as more testing walks for the energetic), the law is fairly similar. The Department of Highways, Ports and Properties is responsible for maintaining the rights of way which have been recorded on a definitive map. Many footpath and waymarking signs have been erected. The authority publishes a very readable 'Public Rights of Way and Outdoor Leisure' map to a scale of 1:25 000 based on the definitive map. Several long-distance footpaths have been established by the authority.

When it could be claimed that Scotland has the most civilized legal system in the world, it is odd that the position on public rights of way is unsatisfactory there. In this superb walking country there is no definitive map giving

58

legal and conclusive evidence of the existence of rights of way as in England and Wales. A path there has a legal standing only when it can be proved to have had uninterrupted use for twenty years 'openly and peaceably'. Some planning authorities have made maps showing the existence of rights of way in their areas, but the maps have no legal standing.

The OS and Bartholomew's maps of Scotland show footpaths and tracks, but it is not made clear whether or not they are rights of way. One cannot expect to see signposts, since no one has the responsibility for signposting rights of way. A planning authority *may* do so, but there is no obligation. The Scottish Rights of Way Society has erected hundreds of signs, but these are a drop in the ocean. Consequently, in using the footpaths in Scotland, a walker is usually stepping into unknown territory and can only assume that he is on a right of way unless he has evidence to the contrary. A Scottish landowner has no obligation to maintain rights of way through his land but, in theory, if the way is dangerous and its condition causes an accident, he could be sued! The public has the right however to go along the path and make repairs and erect stiles, and remove obstructions, so long as the action does not affect the landowner's interests. Planning authorities can also make repairs if they wish.

The Scottish planning authorities, usually District Councils, have the duty to assert and protect the rights of way and can create new ones. Any complaints can be made to them. The Countryside Commission for Scotland can also, with agreement from the Secretary of State, create new foot-paths, and have notably so created some fine long-distance routes: the West Highland Way, the Southern Upland Way and the Speyside Way. One day Scotland may rationalize its rights-of-way system; the longer it leaves the task, the more difficult it will become.

The position is similar in Ireland, where there is no clear up-to-date legislation on public rights of way. Since 1964 the County Councils have powers to make rights of way, but have seldom used them except to secure access to beaches.

However, it is not very likely that a walker will be turned off an existing path in the real countryside even if there is no right of passage. Genuine walkers are welcome! The Irish National Sports Council, with the cooperation of government departments, landowners and environmental groups, has produced some very fine long-distance routes. These routes are waymarked, but not obtrusively.

In Northern Ireland the District Councils have the responsibility for asserting and protecting the public rights of way. They can create new paths by agreement or by an order, and can cooperate to produce long-distance routes. Northern Ireland's Access to the Countryside Order was only made law in 1983, and it seems that there is a long way to go here before one can see the necessary improvements – for instance, in signposting and waymarking.

There may be rights on pedestrian highways, but there are also responsibilities. If one has to open a gate on a public right of way, it should be closed after passage. The short advice in the general Country Code on official leaflets and in publications advises 'close all gates', but this needs qualification. Sometimes on a route a farmer has propped open a gate to allow stock to circulate between two fields; he is going to be irritated if his stock has a restricted feed because of a well-meaning gate-closer. Gates and stiles should be provided en route, and they should be used. If they do not appear to be there, map-reading could be at fault!

Once the walk is planned over the public rights of way, theoretically there should be no problems. But supposing one goes wrong on the walk and loses the footpath? The walker will then most probably be trespassing. If in extricating himself the walker climbs over a fence or wall, he must take very good care not to cause any damage. The accidental removal of the capping stones ('cams') from a wall can let in the weather and cause a wall collapse. This is serious nowadays, when there is little labour available to make repairs, and a damager can be sued.

An offence is committed if a walker is foolish enough to refuse to leave private land by the shortest route, on the landowner's request.

What about bulls in fields crossed by footpaths? The somewhat messy law in England, Wales and Scotland is a masterpiece of the committee system of drafting legislation and the British genius for compromise. As one who once had to make a burst of speed to race an impressive bovine antagonist to a gate, which could well have qualified me for a place in the Olympics, the subject is dear to my heart.

In a nutshell, the law in England, Wales and Scotland states that it is legal for a farmer to put a bull in a field crossed by a right of way, conditional on it being under eleven months old; or a bull being of a recognized *beef, not a dairy*, breed, *and accompanied by cows or heifers*. Any walker should be able to perceive at once if a bull is a juvenile – I am sure that we need not go into that delicate detail – but one might need to memorize a breed recognition chart to identify the dairy breeds officially listed as: Ayrshire, British Friesian, British Holstein, Dairy Shorthorn, Guernsey, Jersey, and Kerry. (Watch this space, the E.E.C. might hatch some other breeds.) If it is at all helpful, I can tell you that the bull which very effectively disputed my legal right to use a public footpath through its field was a British Friesian, which is easily distinguishable: it is black and white. At the time I did not know the drill. Walkers who come across one of the dairy bulls on a public footpath should stare it directly in the eyes and tell it that under the Wildlife and Countryside Act of 1981 its presence is an offence. It should then make an embarrassed retreat.

The question is – is it right to assume that a beef bull with cows is docile? Generally, yes. I know of one large field in a popular tourist area which is traversed by hundreds of walkers daily in the season. Many of them are not even aware that the bull is there, though it is a massive animal. Sometimes when it is only a few feet from the footpath it disdains to even glance at the walkers, even those with dogs. Beef bulls can sometimes be seen being led on to show fields by little girls in pretty dresses. However, it is something of a problem when a docile bull is leaning its considerable tonnage nonchalantly on a gate which one is trying to open.

It can be generally assumed that beef bulls with cows

need cause little concern. However, I once asked my local vet what he thought. Being a canny Scot, he took some time to reply, measuring his words carefully. 'Put it this way,' he suggested, 'a dairy bull is quicker off the mark than a beef bull.'

Seriously, one must have some sympathy for the farmer. Originally the law prohibited the placing of any bulls in fields crossed by rights of way, and as one once required to enforce this law, I must say that I appreciated the farmers' dilemma. It restricted the economical use of his holding severely, and fencing to a small farmer was prohibitively expensive. The revised law gives him some welcome freedom, and I have not heard in recent years of any farmer running a dairy bull in a field with a right of way. If the law is not working somewhere, then this should be publicized.

What about off-putting 'Beware of the Bull' notices? Where they appear at or on a public right of way, they could be said to be illegal, and any present should be reported to the highway authority. A farmer has no right to put a bull of any breed into a field crossed by a public path, knowing or suspecting that the bull could be a danger; that would be utterly irresponsible. In England and Wales he would be in breach of Health and Safety at Work laws, and the Animals Act, and would deserve prosecution.

In Ireland, Northern Ireland and the Isle of Man, bulls may be encountered on public paths, but if they dispute the walkers' right to be there too it might or might not be comforting to know that the bull's owner may be in breach of the law, or could be liable for damages. No landowner has the right to put the public at risk.

LONG-DISTANCE FOOTPATHS

With the cooperation of landowners, a number of long-distance footpaths have been secured by the Countryside Commission, the Countryside Commission for Scotland, Cospoir (the Irish National Sports Council) the Countryside and Wildlife Branch of the Department of the Environment for Northern Ireland, and the Isle of Man Highway and Transport Board. It is *not* necessary to be a long-distance walker to enjoy most of them, for in the majority of cases they can be joined and left at numerous points. Indeed most long-distance paths, by their nature, must have some stretches that are less attractive than other lengths, and taking the attractive bites out of them can be rewarding. Do not assume that it is necessary to graduate to a long-distance expedition: do what you want to do.

One virtue of established long-distance footpaths is that they are unlikely to be obstructed. A list of long-distance paths is shown in Appendix 1.

OPEN COUNTRY
A public right of way might lead on to that open country where walkers are free to walk where they will. This can be fell country in the north, or downs in the south, or it could be heath, or moor or mountain anywhere. More often than not, public access on the land will be by let and not by right. The land could be common land.

Common land in England and Wales, like most other land, is generally privately owned: by individuals, or by councils, companies or corporate bodies. Legally, in most rural areas, unless there is a change in the laws, the general public have no *right* of access; for 'common land' only means that the commoners of the area around have certain rights on the land in common, often dating back to time immemorial and jealously guarded: for instance, the rights to graze their animals or their geese. In practice the general public might not be excluded from the land; but the commoners can be excused if they get indignant about privileges being abused, such as vehicles being driven on to the land, dogs loose among stock, the lighting of picnic fires and the leaving of litter.

The Law of Property Act of 1925 gives right of public access on commons in urban areas (which might include a lot of countryside). In the case of some rural common lands a local authority, a National Park, the National Trust or the National Trust for Scotland may have ownership or management responsibilities; or the owner of a common might have entered into a deed of access dedicating it for the purpose of recreation, but subject to regulating by-laws. In these cases the land is available to walkers.

The law on commons is in urgent need of revision. Common land has been lost and abused over the centuries, and the process continues. It makes sense that subject to their care and maintenance the public should have free access over them.

Although the public might have enjoyed access over some moorland or mountain from time immemorial, this does not necessarily convey a *right*. The matter might be academic if one could wander about at will anyway, but on private open uncultivated land the freedom might be legitimately restricted at certain times, say at lambing time in spring, or in summer during grouse shooting or, particularly in Scotland, at deer-stalking times (1 August to 20 October).

National Parks in England and Wales, the Countryside Commission for Scotland, the District Councils in Northern Ireland, the National Parks and Monuments Service of the Office of Public Works in Ireland – all have powers to secure 'Access Agreements', or to acquire land in open country. Where this power has been exercised the public have right of access, subject to by-laws. Such access land is marked on up-to-date maps, and one would hope to see signs at entrance points.

In Ireland there is generally freedom to roam on all the hills and mountains. On the Isle of Man most of the high moorland and glens are owned by the Manx government and there is much freedom of access; there, open land available to the public is shown on the island's map splendidly as 'areas of public ramblage'! (One might hope that the ways are not hindered by too much bramblage?)

NATIONAL PARKS

National Parks are places preserved for their special scenic qualities, but also for their public enjoyment, particularly for walkers. Although most of the walking might be done near home, sooner or later you must savour the pleasures of walking in areas which have been designated to protect the superb landscapes for which they are famous; in England and Wales these amount to over 10 per cent of the land: Dartmoor, Exmoor, Pembrokeshire Coast, Brecon Beacons, Snowdonia, the Peak District, the Yorkshire Dales, the Lake District, North Yorks Moors, and Northumberland, (in effect) the Broads, and the New Forest.

Here, unlike most National Parks in other countries, the park authorities do not own all the land within their boundaries. They are special planning authorities and they have three statutory duties: (1) to preserve and enhance the natural beauty of the area; (2) to promote its enjoyment by the public; and (3) to have regard for the social and economic well-being of the inhabitants. So the Parks not only have a duty to oversee the rights-of-way system, (in some the responsibility for rights-of-way maintenance has been delegated to them by the highway authority), but to secure access to their open country. They can do this by negotiating an Access Agreement with their local land-owners; and if necessary can make an Access Order. In areas subject to such agreements or orders, or on open land dedicated for public enjoyment owned by authorities or the National Trust, one has freedom to roam, subject to protective by-laws. In other open areas in National Parks there is often free access, but not necessarily by right.

Scotland has much of the most beautiful and exciting landscapes in the British Isles, but although a governmental Scottish National Parks Survey Committee in 1945 recommended the creation of five National Parks there was no action taken. There are still (1992) no National Parks in Scotland, for reasons that are very hard to understand. A Scottish Countryside Commission was established in 1967 with a duty to provide for the preservation of Scotland's superb landscapes and to ensure the provision of facilities for their enjoyment. In 1974 the Commission produced a report for government entitled *A Park System for Scotland*. At long last were we to have National Parks, benefiting from the experience and the mistakes of the system in England and Wales? Something sensibly and uniquely

65

Scottish? Not at all! The report promoted the establishment of 'Urban Parks', 'Country Parks', 'Regional Parks' and 'Special Parks'; and later, 'National Scenic Areas'.

However, there followed promising signs! In 1989 the Scottish Minister for Home Affairs invited the Countryside Commission for Scotland to make a further review of the management arrangements for popular mountain areas, and the Commission's recommendations (late 1990) were that areas of the Cairngorms, Loch Lomond, Ben Nevis/Glencoe/Black Mount, and Wester Ross should be designated as National Parks. A survey (*System Three Scotland*, published by the Countryside Commission, April 1991) showed that 84 per cent of the population were in favour of a National Park system for Scotland. Yet, so far, government has declined to act on the advice.

Whatever happens, access to most of the open country in Scotland is traditional, and given a continuance of good will by landowners, and responsible use by walkers, in theory there should be few problems. The Countryside Commission, which merged with the Nature Conservancy Council for Scotland in 1992 to form Scottish National Heritage, has the authority to come to Access Agreements.

In Northern Ireland there are surprisingly no National Parks either, but the District Councils can secure access to open country, the quiet captivating beauty of which is generally unknown to the vast majority of walkers outside the province; and the Countryside and Wildlife Branch of the Department of the Environment has responsibility for the care of Areas of Outstanding Natural Beauty, National Nature Reserves, and County Parks, and it provides the necessary information about them. Notably it has the care of and the promotion of access to the delectable Mourne Mountains area, which surely deserves National Park status.

Ireland has vast areas of quiet open country, a paradise for walkers, but some of the best has been secured through the acquisition by the National Parks and Monuments Service of three nationally owned and very beautiful National Parks: Killarney, Connemara, and Glenveagh.

One should assume that all the National Parks and the larger areas officially available to the public in the British Isles include, by their very nature, much wild and remote land. There are bound to be many footpath routes on easy ground; however, large areas of the terrain might be regarded as potentially hazardous to inexperienced walkers and much of it is for specialized hill walkers. Hill-walking is dealt with in Chapter 13.

The National Parks have a duty to inform the public about their areas, including advice on walking, and literature is available for the asking.

OTHER ACCESS LAND

Other authorities sometimes offer public access to some of their land; among them at this moment are water supply authorities. In National Parks this is often in agreement with the park service. The Forestry Commission in England, Wales and Scotland, and the State Forests in Ireland, now allow walkers on their land. The National Trust, the National Trust for Scotland and An Taisce (Ireland's National Trust) – which in spite of the 'national' title are not statutory authorities but private charities – own large and small tracts of beautiful land in open country, sea-shore and park land to most of which the public have access. In some cases, particularly park land, there could be a charge for admission. Where the trusts own farms, obviously there will be some access restrictions.

Country Parks have been established in England and Wales with the support of the Countryside Commission. Located around populated areas, their prime object is to attract country-goers and take the pressure off the sensitive areas of National Parks. In fact some provide valuable walking opportunities. The Countryside Commission for Scotland has also helped to establish Country Parks; most of them have ranger services and there are programmes of guided walks.

Nature reserves are very varied. Some are owned by statutory authorities, some by the county's Wildlife Trust. One should expect to have to ask for a permit to enter and, having entered, to observe the rules. For instance, it might be necessary to keep strictly to footpaths. This is fair enough if the vegetation is to be conserved; and once animals and birds on the reserve have become accustomed to people using the footpaths they are less likely to be disturbed and are more easily seen. Garish clothing should not be worn. Dogs are not normally allowed, or must be on a lead. It is not usually necessary to creep about in a nature reserve, but quietness is appreciated.

It should not be too hard to seek out, and plan to use, these places where there is freedom to walk. Plan the day well, but not *so* well that the plan becomes a tyranny. Accept that it is a bad plan that admits of no modification: 'The best laid schemes o' mice an' men gang aft agley'. When the plan goes 'agley' it need not be a catastrophe; this could be when the real adventure starts.

8

Technique

When walking up a steep on to the Coullins on the Isle of Skye I met two nervous people resting, having abandoned a climb, and one remarked, 'We could tell you're an experienced mountaineer because you're walking upright. We had to come up here on all fours!'

I was surprised. I could never call myself an experienced mountaineer; but a walker . . . yes. A walker does not walk on all fours! After a deal of experience in walking, the magical body machine finds out for itself the way to least effort. One way on a slope is to keep in upright balance. An upright stance is safest and easiest. It is a mistake to dig in the toes and lean too far forward; using the hands is only necessary on a very steep rough scramble – around 20 degrees from vertical – which has not a lot to do with country walking. To lean too far forward means that the toe-holds can slip out and a face-down collapse is possible.

Standing more upright, however, and bending the foot at the ankle means that the boots' well-cleated soles and heels are flat on the surface, providing maximum friction grip. Exceptionally, say in steep snow, it might be advisable to kick in the toes or the sides of the boots, but even then it is necessary to remain upright. A good balance can be cultivated, and placing the foot for effective grip should also come naturally. On some uneven surfaces, or often on a slippery surface too, it is necessary to walk flat-footed; this moves the body's centre of gravity on to the whole foot and gives the boot soles and heels the maximum grip.

RHYTHM
If one watches a person long experienced with walking on varying terrain – a shepherd perhaps (there are still many of them who do not do their shepherding on motor-cycles!) – it

will be seen that there is no stiffness about the gait. The legs are slightly bent, the whole body is used, the forward movement of each leg is aided by a slight swing of the hips. It is not exactly a ballet movement, but it is elegant enough. The adoption of that loose movement saves fatigue and muscle strain.

After practice the body can develop an easy, natural rhythm, which of course varies with the individual's normal length of stride and natural speed. Being aware of the rhythm and keeping to it means there is much less effort required, tiredness is evaded and one is better able to enjoy the environment.

A rhythm can be acquired; it can also be imposed. When armies went on foot, not for nothing did they march to the beat of a pipe and drum, or full-blown bands playing marching tunes. Once they moved as one, the pounding of synchronized boots accentuated the beat and long distances could be covered without undue weariness. The imposed corporate rhythm became part of the discipline, and it sealed the bond of the unit.

But an imposed rhythm is not as effective as the cultivation of a body's natural one, which can be reached quite unconsciously after repeated practice. Once acquired it is possible to use it to advantage, easing into it deliberately when necessary from time to time, picking it up, as regular as the beat of a metronome, counting to it, or humming a tune to it until it is slipped into effortlessly, without too much further thought. Then the rhythm of the leg swing hardly varies. Going on the level, uphill or downhill, accelerating or slowing, it is only a matter of shortening or lengthening the stride to continue the rhythm. It is a shift of gear: like a finely-tuned engine at its peak, the body is working at its most effective pitch, with each muscle acting in resonance with all. It is a natural flow which becomes second nature and from practice walking can become a joy. On an ascent other walkers may overtake and pass, but the odds are that you will come across them later, sitting to regain breath and strength, while you will need no rest.

FOOT CARE

Something should be said here about foot care. Feet not used to sustained walking can get sore, but the possibility is minimized if the boots are a good fit and the socks soft. However, if the skin needs hardening the old remedy is to treat them with methylated spirit the night before. (It used to be whisky when the life-giving liquid was reasonably priced – oh, happy days!) Or there are two other methods – the redolent, and the pungent: (*1*) rub the feet all over with lemon peel; or, (*2*) take a tip from the ancient Roman army if you dare – they rubbed their feet with raw onion or garlic!

When the feet are washed before the walk they should be thoroughly dried and then – just before getting socked and booted – they might be dusted with foot powder or talcum powder. If the walk is likely to be wet underfoot it is a good idea to stuff a spare pair of socks in the pack; then wet socks can be swapped for dry during the course of the journey. Walking for too long in wet socks can cause soreness.

If a blister is raised and becomes painful, it should be gently burst and dressed. The technique is to use a clean needle or pin (sterilized by placing the point in a match flame). The blister should be punctured at one *side*, and the fluid gently squeezed out. With an adhesive dressing applied to cover the area, all should be well and one can walk on comfortably.

When on the walk, the temptation to plunge tired and hot feet into a cooling stream should be resisted, unless there is only a short distance still to go; otherwise, further progress might be uncomfortable. An alternative is to try an ancient remedy. On the banks of the cooling stream some alder trees ought to be growing. Alder favours wet areas and has a dark trunk and round or oval leaves. According to Culpeper, the famous seventeenth-century physician, 'The leaves put under the bare feet galled with travelling are a great refreshment to them.' Clogs were made (and are still) of alder wood, which maybe explains why they are so cool and comfortable for pottering about – not for walking! Alder is one of my favourite trees as it grows where most

71

others will not. I have planted thousands of them, but must admit I have never tried the foot remedy.

After the walk, tired feet can be soothed luxuriously in a footbath containing camomile, or sprigs of peppermint or lavender.

SPEED
What about walking speed? Most will walk with companions or with the family at a mutually acceptable rate, with consideration given to the less able members. This is not always easy, and if walking speeds are incompatible, friendship can come under strain; it is a matter of give and take. I am sure from the evidence of my own ears that lovers' relationships are often threatened, perhaps sometimes broken almost irrevocably, when the male partner tries to project a macho image by demonstrating his superior strength as a walker, urging on his poor, frailer partner who is struggling painfully behind. It is worse still if he then gets them both lost and the couple have to trudge a further unnecessary 5 miles or so. (If the relationship is a permanent one, the incident might well be brought up in many future domestic disagreements!)

On the other hand, happy are they who can seal their bond in a successful walking partnership, synchronizing their progress, if not their individual rhythm, and sharing the experience naturally with no need to sustain continual conversation.

WHO WITH?
There are naturally social beings who would choose to walk with a group, and there are many active rambling and walking clubs. However, it is a pity if the sociable aim of the group takes a very superior role at the expense of the full appreciation of the countryside. Stopping to enjoy a view, to observe birds, to examine flowers, or even to take a photograph can sometimes be difficult if a walker has to keep up with his party.

The larger clubs offer a choice of 'A', 'B', or 'C' parties with distances and terrains graded to suit abilities and preferences, and that is good. Much depends on the quality of the leadership. A bad party leader may suffer a working week of abject slavery and at weekends may want to reverse the role as well as prove his prowess. It could then be a case of 'head down, eyes front, keep going, and don't dare stop' – not for anything, not even a desire to answer the call of nature, for catching up might be impossible. There is also a tendency for male members of the club who would be happier in the less testing 'B' or 'C' groups to consider it a slight on their manhood if they decline to go with the 'A'! To their cost! New members can decide by experiment which group suits them best.

One disadvantage of walking with an organized club is that there might be little opportunity to enjoy self-navigation. The leaders plan the route and it is only necessary to follow. Some club members may never see a map, and at the end of the day have only a vague idea of where they have been.

I do not wish to be unduly critical of walking clubs, particularly Ramblers Association clubs. I have met and walked happily with many, and there are some excellent leaders. Social activity is very necessary, even vital, to a lot of people, and it is doubly enjoyable if it is in the open air. Some single women are quite understandably nervous about walking alone, and it is natural for them to join a club. Many club members have a lifetime of happy experiences and live for the weekends. But to get the maximum from a club walk, its members must surely be aware that the primary object is the enjoyment of the countryside. It troubles me to hear an elderly life-time dedicated club member tell me that he has never seen a wild deer, though they thrive within 20 miles of his home on terrain he must have crossed and re-crossed a thousand times.

GUIDED WALKS

Many organizations, tourist authorities, National Parks, Country Parks, Ramblers Association groups, local Wild-life Trusts and other voluntary organizations run pro-grammes of guided walks. It is possible to learn a lot from a leader who knows his subject and enthuses about it, and some such walks are especially good as a novice's introduction to country walking.

Guided walks vary in quality. Some are excellent, some fair, and unfortunately many are very poor. It is not enough for a leader to be an expert. He has to be a good communicator with a good voice, and an understanding that he must gather all his clients about him each time he gives his talk, for no one should be left out. A guided walk leader needs training and experience for it is a very skilled job. But even when well trained, much depends on the personality of the leader. It is possible to be led around a historic city by guides with identical training and dedication, and while one of them may instantly seize and sustain attention – noticing and responding to the reactions of his clients, talking to them at their level, leavening the information with the right measure of lightness and humour, telling a tale with a natural flow and emphasis – another may have the same basic spiel but will lack that skill that draws concentration, that rarer compelling mysticism of the natural story-teller.

Alas, some guides, professional as well as volunteer, no matter how enthusiastic, are so programmed to a planned walk route and information that they have little conception of the needs, abilities and interests of their customers. Some routes might strain walkers too far, even place them in potential danger. The leader should not always call the tune.

There is a boom in commercially-run guided walks, and 'activity holidays' are becoming very popular. Some are long established and reliable, but there are others whose credentials might need examination. I remember being approached by a well-equipped fell-walker in a large (I discovered later, commercially organized) party, on Great Gable's summit. The day had patchy drifts of low cloud but was then very clear. 'Could you tell me the way to Sty Head?' he asked. I pointed out the easily seen route but suggested to him that if he wanted to identify the landmarks his leader would surely explain. He beamed cheerfully at me. 'I am the leader.'

There is really no way of assessing the competence of a leader even by looking closely at him or her. That suitably confidence-giving open-air tan, the country gear and the eyes gleaming with enthusiasm may mask a complete fool. The walker seeking an 'activity holiday' must make sure that he is buying what he needs: between the extremes of muscle-straining, 'character-building' 'outward bound' experience, and the easy countryside strolls. If the organizers do not seem to know the difference, they should be given a wide berth!

Some natural history societies have study walks, and a great deal can be learned from enthusiastic practical naturalists which cannot be fully assimilated from books. It is hardly possible to learn to identify birds, for instance, without walking with knowledgeable experts who can recognize a species in silhouette; how often can one be sure of colour? or of the song or cry? With nature walks informality is the thing, with plenty of time for looking and asking questions. Groups of no more than, say, fifteen, are essential, and some party discipline is needed if there is to be quiet observation of wildlife. I strongly recommend everyone interested in the countryside to join a local wild-life trust, or natural history society; their organized walks can teach a lot and can point one in the right direction to follow a preferred interest. No greater knowledge is asked for on the walks; novices are always welcome.

A DOG?

A dog is a great companion on a walk, but its presence puts a burden of control on its owner. Untrained dogs – and untrained owners – are not going to be comfortable in the countryside. A dog is a responsibility: no one should own one unless he intends to train it. I am a firm believer in dog owners and their dogs attending dog-training classes. At the very least a dog should come to heel at once when called; it should drop, and 'stay' on command, and walk to heel. The secret of training is to deal firmly with refusals of command and, most important, praise lavishly on obedience.

The number-one complaint of farmers about visitors is

'dogs out of control'. If dogs are unaccustomed to seeing sheep, curiosity might prompt a loose dog to investigate, then the sheep runs and a chase develops. A flock can then panic; pregnant ewes can lose their lambs; sheep can be driven into watercourses. At worse an over-excited dog, even a normal friendly pet, can respond to some aroused hunting instinct and attack. The moral is to keep dogs on leads when passing through farm stock. I advise this even though a dog might be trained to walk to heel lead-less, since it will at least save the observing farmer a dangerous rise in blood pressure. A dog owner who has no proper control of his dog when crossing through enclosed land containing sheep can, in England and Wales, be prosecuted even though his dog makes no move towards the sheep. In any case, if a farmer sees a dog on his sheep pasture chasing or worrying sheep, or has reason to believe that it might do so, he has the right to shoot the dog and prosecute the owner. Dog-loving farmers would say that they would prefer to shoot the owner and prosecute the dog!

Dogs are normally banned from nature reserves, though some do allow them on leads. In forests where there are deer, dogs should be on leads or on lines. Walkers who do not heed this rule can lose their dogs for hours, for dogs are naturally excited at the scent of deer, few can resist a chase and they are deaf to calls and whistles. My sympathy is wholly with the deer.

Incidentally, dog owners are quite within their rights to take controlled dogs along rights of way, where 'No Dogs' signs have no legality. I know of one nature reserve where dogs are banned on their made routes; but a right of way passes through it and dog owners, with dogs on leads, walk regularly along it and there is nothing to prevent them.

One problem of which dog owners should be aware is that passing through a field occupied by *cows with calves* can be hazardous. If one cow thinks that the dog, though it be on a lead, is a threat to her calf, she can react and start a general protective panic in the herd. Once, faced with an aggressive stampede started by such a situation, I picked up my heavy German Shepherd dog (which was not in the least apprehensive) and threw it over a wall into the next field. Unknown strength often comes from crisis!

I have never been long without a dog. They are fantastic companions; they do not argue with you; they are not perturbed if you lose your way (though one terrier companion I had got very uppish if I had to retrace my steps). Watch a dog using its nose and its ears, and you can notice things you would otherwise miss. Dogs not only can urge one on with their exuberance when muscles flag; they can be particularly closely affectionate when covered with mud, or when you open the packed lunch.

ALONE?

Solitary walking cannot be everyone's choice, though more often than not it would be mine. There are two things that modern humankind avoids – solitude and quietness. Man is a gregarious animal; few are generally comfortable when too long out of reach of human contact. To most people solitude is equated with aloneness and is only to be endured when it sneaks up on the unprepared – particularly in the feared inevitability – in physical pain and illness. And quietness is equated perhaps with a kind of creeping nothingness; then what dreadful spectres crawl out of that empty darkness! Push it back with conversation – turn on the radio!

But to some there is a vast difference between loneliness and solitude, and there is a wonderful eloquence in the quietness of the countryside. Undisturbed by company, a solitary walker can more easily reach that awareness of all around that speaks to the senses. At best it can lead to an inward journey into *self*-awareness: that which the hermit seeks in his cell, the wise man in the wilderness.

Or perhaps the solitary walker seeks no depths of feeling, but rather a cap-in-the-air sense of freedom! No need for the distraction of conversation. No need to match pace with someone else. Freedom to journey as far or as little as you please without seeking agreement. Freedom to detour, retrace, to sit still long enough to overcome the caution of wild creatures, to take a long, long look – as long as you please. To stop and soak up the sun; to eat and drink when you want. To not feel guilty or apologetic when you miss the way, and to congratulate yourself for being no end of a fellow when you find it again. To pretend that you are the only person in the world and don't need to care a damn for anyone else, or anyone's opinion of you!

Females particularly may feel nervous about walking alone, especially in remote countryside. If so, and they do have a taste for solitude, then they must seek like-minded company – walkers, not talkers. Given compatibility, and at the sacrifice of only a little freedom, it is possible for two to enjoy solitude together; even three to enjoy three, or four four! But there should be a pact of quietness.

Quietness makes a lot of difference. I once shared a long and happy, very quiet country walk with twelve others – all deaf and dumb. We drew attention to occasional landscape features, to flowers and birds, to shared surprise and happiness, with eye contact and with touch. The countryside experience was all. How much enjoyment is deflected and drowned in all-too-easy continual conversation?

I will allow though that the walk's enjoyment is enhanced by a chance chat with encountered fellow walkers, or a local friendly countryman with time to talk about his patch. And of course even the preferred lone walker must occasionally enjoy congenial company. However easy it is to put the world to rights – everything is seen in the right perspective when completely relaxed, leaning on a gate! But make it a rule never – *never* – to talk about work. Forget the work-day occupation; the soul of country walking is emancipation.

A COUNTRYSIDE CODE

It is hardly possible to enjoy the countryside without showing responsibility. Every country walker must be a conservationist, which of course means guarding against risk of fire. Thankfully no one lights picnic fires nowadays, but in my experience most fires in the countryside are caused by picnic stoves, or smokers' carelessly discarded lighted matches or fag-ends. The most dangerous time for fires is after a dry spell in early spring, before the new green growth puts on a protective moist cover. But fires caused by carelessness can happen at any time and some areas are especially vulnerable – heather moorland for instance; and if the fire gets into underlying peat it can burn for days or weeks. However, it would be wrong to assume that a heather fire is always accidental. It is necessary to have a controlled burning of heather to maintain its cover, and grouse moor owners must burn occasionally too. Otherwise any sign of fires starting, particularly in forest areas, should be reported with a 999 call. An early attack on it can save horrendous damage.

Like park rangers in other areas of Britain I have been involved in the terrible business of fire-fighting, and the frustrating and time-consuming job of trying to kill a peat fire, which usually means digging as well as beating. Ninety-nine point nine per cent of the fires are caused by someone's carelessness. There is little else that can cause greater damage and anger.

If a walk crosses farm land, it should be recognized that it is in a working area and livestock should not be unduly disturbed. The walk should keep to the footpaths; if it goes through a closed gate, this should be shut again after passing.

Plants, wildlife and trees should be protected. If one is anxious to identify a plant it should not be plucked unless it is very prolific. Sometimes it is the keen botanists who are the main culprits here!

Countrygoers once felt it necessary to record their presence by carving their initials on a tree. This is graffiti of the worst type, for it cannot be cleaned off. Moreover, it also wounds the tree.

Wild creatures should be left alone. I have lived most of my life in an area where roe deer are common. Many tiny fawns meet their death at the hands of well-meaning people who find the creature curled up in undergrowth and, thinking it abandoned by its mother, pick it up. The fact is that the mother – the roe doe – aware that its presence could be scented and might attract predators while the fawn itself has little scent, places its offspring in cover and leaves it, returning at intervals at feeding times. Once the fawn is handled and bears human scent the doe will not recognize it as its own and will abandon it. The orphan will then die of starvation.

Any young creature found should *not* be handled. It should not be assumed that it is neglected. Mum might be nearer than you think!

Birds' nests too are sometimes abandoned when disturbed by photographers. Some bird species are especially vulnerable and one should always be sensitive. It is of course illegal to disturb the nests of protected birds.

Sometimes living things are killed because they look threatening, but *nothing* should be killed unnecessarily. Adders have their purpose and are harmless if left alone; regretably the slow-worm, which is really a legless lizard and feeds only on insects, is often killed by people who think it is a 'nasty snake'. Moths – of any species – are often killed 'because they destroy clothing'. There are hundreds of moth species in the countryside and their larvae feed only on leaves and plants. Many of them have great beauty, and should be admired, and left alone.

Watercourses often constitute water supplies to rural communities, though sometimes this may seem hard to understand. A group of cottages might be within a mile or so of a large reservoir providing for some urban population. Yet their own drinking water will be piped from a spring – or a dammed pool in a stream which might be tempting for a secluded swim on a hot day. It is sad that unpleasant experiences have compelled the erection of barbed-wire fences round some picturesque rural water supplies!

Surely it should not be necessary to ask anyone to keep the countryside tidy. But, it is hardly possible to walk very far in the country without seeing the evidence of someone's nastiness. This is not thoughtlessness, for someone who has discarded a drink must have thought, 'I have finished the drink and I don't want its empty container'. It is a gesture of contempt for the countryside.

I remember a naturalist who was helping to clear up the mess left by visitors assuring me that educating people towards tidiness would be an uphill struggle. For dropping litter, he assured me, was instinctive, the human male marking his territory. 'Animals,' he assured me, 'do it with urine and excreta or scent glands. The human does it with his cigarette packet or his beer can.' But dropping litter is certainly not the male prerogative, and no one can really appreciate the extent of the problem until he has been on litter sweeps.

Nothing, not even a sweet wrapper, should mark one's passage.

It is hardly possible to plan a walk which, at some time, does not use a country road which by its nature is narrow and winding. This is a serious hazard on any walk. Although the advice often given is to always walk facing the oncoming traffic, I suggest that this could be a dangerous practice without qualification. It is good advice if the road has verges which offer refuge; but country roads are often without verges and are bounded by banks, hedges and walls. There is no escape, therefore it is necessary for vehicle drivers to see the walkers as far as possible ahead. That means walkers facing oncoming traffic, but using the *outside of bends*, even though that also involves the need to keep crossing the road with great care. Strangely, some motorists do not seem to understand that pedestrians have a right of passage on a carriage road, and rather than stop when overtaking the walkers – if balked momentarily by oncoming traffic – will pin the unfortunates into the hedge.

Of course, when behind the wheel myself I do sometimes think that *some* pedestrians take up far too much of the road and ought to show some consideration to country folk who are trying to get on with their work . . .

Many – sometimes I think most – motorists drive too fast on country lanes. This is foolish. There could be a rambling club or a flock of sheep around that next bend. Wild animals and birds are all too often casualties through thoughtlessness. The trouble is that the modern motor vehicle has been designed to cruise at its happiest around 50-plus miles per hour, which compels its driver to feel uncomfortable at anything less.

AWARENESS

Most of us have to work to a routine. We exist by habit; routine becomes a comforting tranquillizer. For most of the time, we are sleep-walking and can hardly recall a memorable event from one working day to the next. What we have to do on a country walk is to get rid of that soporific fog that still fuddles the brain even when it begins to be stirred by the sight of unaccustomed scenery. We must take some good deep breaths and come alive.

We must first overcome a handicap. Seeing always involves a not-seeing and we have to choose an area of attention from the countryside's bombardment of visual stimuli. In the eighteenth and early nineteenth centuries the countrygoing aesthetic did not seek to appreciate the rural scenery in the raw. He or she would carry a 'claud glass', a small convex mirror in a pretty frame about the size of a pocket-book. It was then necessary to stand with one's back to the view, hold up the glass and look at its picture image which could be moved about until the balance of its elements was just right. The aim was to capture a classical framed Arcadian picture reminiscent of the works of the popular Italian painter, Claude Lorraine (hence 'claud glass').

Smile not at the eccentricities of our forebears, for we still have our claud glasses. Perhaps most of us nowadays are happy to see the country scene within the frame of a television screen, in the comfort of home, sterilized and deodorized in one simple dimension. At best it can be an incentive to break out and experience the real thing. At worst it is a tawdry substitute.

So here we are in the countryside, comfortably dressed, equipped, and with a planned excursion in mind. There remains a need for awareness: to awaken the mind and senses. Alas, as we grow older, without our knowing, our senses – so well tuned in youth – tend to become atrophied from disuse. They need regular exercise; we must drag them out of their dim cells into the light and fresh air! To enter the kingdom, one must again be as a little child.

Ideally, it is a matter of approaching the experience as if for the very first time. For those who are not too self-conscious about trying an experiment, here it is. From a comfortable position overlooking a pleasing country scene – perhaps while leaning on a tree – close your eyes for a few moments and try to wipe away all thoughts from your mind. Try very hard to think of absolutely nothing. Hold it for at least three minutes; more if you can hold a blank mind longer. Then open your eyes and look again at the scene as if you have never had the gift of sight before. Accept it freely. Drink deep. Open up your perception first to nearby features, then to embrace the whole of the scene. It could be like looking at colour when all before was black and white!

Try it again while sitting, and take a close look at flowers and grass. Close your eyes, wipe out thoughts, hold again, then open up and view those plants as if such things had never previously existed. You may see that every plant, each in its special place, has a new meaning. The whole scene, or a bank of plants, can appeal – as well as to the sight – to those inner stirrings of feelings that are undreamed of, and beyond expression. At first this might be uncomfortable. We live so much in a material world that we could be suspicious of the vague stirrings of emotions that excite impractical people like poets and philosophers.

Nature is the pure inspiration of all art: of painting, of poetry, of music, of classical architecture. We can see that a great picture in a gallery may instantly appeal to the eye, but also has something to say. How much more so in the art of nature! Everything we might see before us in nature has a mystical as well as a physical meaning. In the obvious example of a flower, its physical beauty may attract the eye; but it may also speak to the higher part, the spirit. The outward form is the manifestation of life, but the spirit which breathes through all things is its essence.

After a while of practice at opening awareness, it will hardly be necessary to go through an exercise – only a matter of preparing the mind, leaving all disturbing thoughts and feelings behind, opening and expanding the senses, and accepting a new experience at almost every turn. Every walk in the countryside could be an adventure of mind, body and spirit.

9

Walking Close to Home

Discovery can consist of seeing familiar things from an unfamiliar prospect. Behind every known hides the unknown. That commonplace territory on the urban fringe, previously seen only from a car or public transport, becomes an unexplored wilderness, full of surprises, when it is observed from footpath level at 3 miles per hour.

We could easily start walking from our own backyard and be delightfully surprised. The first surprise could come from the opening of a large-scale map of the area showing the rights of way. I remember one resident on the fringe of a town being astonished after he asked if I would show him my map. He had never seen a large-scale map and had no idea that he lived within a network of rights of way, one of them beginning at a narrow stile only a few feet away from his garden wall. For years, any walking he had done had been confined to the roadsides.

In former times, every settlement would have its ancient ways, where residents of old would head for the church – or the inn; or might take their beasts or geese to graze on the common. Later there might have been new routes made, to the railway station, the school, or the shop. These might well be there on the rights-of-way map, and duly copied on to the large-scale maps.

PUBLIC FOOTPATHS
Public footpaths belong to everyone, though it is sometimes argued that old footpaths used by residents to go to the church and shops should not be open to all and sundry for other, recreational uses. However, it could equally be argued that roads made to carry goods to market should not be used for motorists' pleasure trips. Rights of way and highways have the protection of law as rights of passage,

and they are resources that belong to all. There is an old legal maxim: 'once a highways always a highway'.

Walking relatively close to home therefore might mean exploring paths through occupied land, and possibly agricultural areas. This requires some careful map-reading. If you wander off your way in open country there is little problem, whereas walking through occupied land is another matter. In Ireland and Scotland, where there might be no formal rights of way, you could be using a path by courtesy of the landowner.

To give confidence it might be a good idea for an absolute beginner to do the first local expeditions with an organized guided walk, if there is one in the area. But walkers should not get 'hooked' on being taken; they miss out on free enjoyment if they cannot fend for themselves! Some far-seeing district councils and voluntary organizations publish walk leaflets, and they too offer a way to begin. But if walking is to be a regular pastime, it means practicing map-reading at every opportunity.

The countryside of the British Isles has everything – except genuine wilderness – to offer. In the beginning *was* wilderness. What has happened to the landscape since is a record of human history, starting when our Neolithic and Iron Age ancestors made efficient tools and began to axe and burn away that wilderness. Every prospect, if one can read it correctly, has a story to tell. The path or the lane we walk along may date back to ancient Celtic times; it may twist and turn in a peculiar way because it follows old field plans; it may lie in a hollow where in old times banks were thrown up on either side to define landowners' boundaries.

HEDGES

If there are hedges, they always reward scrutiny. Looking at and into hedges is a good excuse to dawdle! Not only are hedges vital habitats for flora and fauna, but the hedge species too are living history. Dr M. D. Hooper, when Senior Scientific Officer for the Nature Conservancy, produced a theory which became known to fellow naturalists as 'Hooper's Hedgerow Hypothesis'. Checking the variety of hedge species with old records, he suggested that the number of species in a sample stretch of 30 yards (27½m) indicated the age of the hedge in centuries. In other words, if a hedge in samples of 30 yards contained, say, hawthorn, holly, blackthorn, elder and hazel, it would be five centuries old. The estimate is amazingly near-accurate, but only really reliable in the South, and parts of the Midlands of England. It is interesting to check it out!

If a hedge is virtually pure old hawthorn, it almost certainly dates back to the Enclosure Acts of last century. To the north and west including Ireland and the Isle of Man, where 'hedges' are sod banks surmounted by shrubs, D. A. Allen, secretary of the Botanical Society of the British Isles, suggested that the number of species of bramble in a given stretch is an age indicator; but the difference in species can only really be recognized by botanists. (The berries all taste the same.)

The flora of a hedge is usually rich and interesting because it contains not only many woodland species, but also the species from the field of which it is the boundary. It also has the climbing plants – that scent of honeysuckle on an evening walk! – and there is often wild rose, old man's beard, the purple vetches and bittersweet. There are plants which favour the feet of hedges – like hedge mustard and woundwort, and the many hogweeds with their foam of white and cream heads.

One can have a lifetime's pleasure in botanical exploration. Alas, some 95 per cent of our flower-meadows have gone, thanks to E.E.C. fertilizers and weed-killers applied in the interest of food production. Thousands of miles of hedgerows have gone too for the same short-term reasons. But where they still exist intact, neglected, or in remnants, they could be a reservoir of wild flowers, and they are good places for botanizing and may well start a lifetime's interest.

The beginner needs a good book. There are many flower identification books on sale – choose one with good colour illustrations. Some such books are published with an eye for the whole European market, and in order to accommodate the large list, some plant species of the British Isles may therefore be omitted. Make sure that the book relates to the British Isles and is comprehensive. A slim volume might fit easily in the pocket, but it is frustrating to find that a quite common species (with its name on the tip of the tongue!) is not included. The book should have a key to help locate the species in need of identification. There are various systems: some keys simply show flower shapes, then indicate the page references; some list them under colours; some do both. However, with gathering knowledge, there may soon be no need to use the book's key. Seeing, for instance, that the flower one needs to identify looks something like a pea flower, one can turn to the section of the book which illustrates the pea family and should find it amongst those pages.

The first rule is: take the book to the plant, not the plant to the book. Plants should not be plucked for identification unless the species is very prolific; it pains me to reiterate that some of the prevalent plant vandalism can be attributed to botanists. If occasionally a flower cannot be found immediately in the book, the drill is to make a sketch of it with a note of the colours and its habitat. It can then be identified at home at leisure.

In former generations when most of the population lived in the countryside, flowers of wayside, meadow and woodland were familiar to all. Their medicinal and their food values were also common knowledge. Some were regarded with superstition, thought to have had magic, or sinister, properties.

To illustrate, let me stroll along an imaginary hedge-side and pick out a few plants. There should be bramble. Blackberries of course were always a valuable fruit and are still gathered by all. In the area where I live they are called deliciously 'bumblykites'! Where I was raised, nice fat juicy ones were called 'dobbers'. According to old superstition they should never ever be picked after Michaelmas Day (this is now 29 September, but used to be in mid-October). I was always told that picking was impossible after Hallowe'en, for on that night the witches spat upon them!

There is invariably elder. In youth, while learning the

trade as a woodman, I was warned never to cut down 'eller', and never to burn it, as bad luck would inevitably follow. I found out later that this superstition is widespread through Europe and Scandinavia. Elder shares with the rowan, or mountain ash, a specially magical reputation; in the fearfully superstitious days, a sprig of it was carried to ward off demons and, because witches were reputedly afraid of it, it was often planted by cottage doors. Like rowan, if it was not growing from the ground but from the rotting hollow of a tree, it had very special magical powers. I was told by a country neighbour that 'everybody knows' that 'eller' growing near a house would keep lightning away. But there were other ancient reasons for valuing its presence. More than any other tree it provided a range of important medicines, some of them almost certainly effective. A decoction of the flowers was used to reduce fever, and cure catarrh, coughs and colds. Cooled, it was employed to treat skin sores and sore eyes. Alternatively, for the same purpose an ointment was made by boiling leaves in mutton fat. The berries were also used to cure fevers, and many other diseases including the rheumatics. But bark and roots were also utilized in a whole host of other remedies. The dried berries were used as currant substitutes in cakes. Nowadays the berries are very often collected to make elderberry wine; and many a countryman and countrylady can recall, after an innocent sampling, the fearful effects of accidental over-indulgence! The flowers, with sugar and lemons, are also used to make refreshing non-alcoholic 'elderflower champagne'.

It used to be thought that everything in nature had been provided by the Creator for the benefit of man. So every single plant had its uses, and the clues for each plant's properties were often clear to see. The spotted leaves of the lungwort (*Pulmonaria officinalis*), for instance, suggested the appearance of a diseased lung; it was therefore useful for chest infections, and it was used for this throughout Europe.

Any red-flowering plant suggested blood, so must have been good to treat wounds. One of those is almost certainly in our hedge – hedge woundwort with its hairy, nettle-like leaves and spike of beetroot-red flowers.

There are certainly members of the cow parsley and hogweed family in the hedge: the *Umbelliferae*, easily recognized by their umbrella-shaped head of flowers, usually white or creamy, held high on hollow stems. They are an attractive, often dominant feature of all hedges. The *Umbelliferae* is a large family and includes one of my favourites, the localized giant hogweed, annually growing from nothing with a stem like a sapling and a height of around 10 feet. It has the reputation of staining the skin permanently if the sap is touched when it is cut, and for that reason is much destroyed. One other of the family – the ground elder – is the scourge of gardeners. The seeds of one of the most common, cow parsley itself, can be used as a flavouring herb, but I have always let well alone as some of its cousins in the family are very poisonous plants, including hemlock; and when scything any of them I dislike the sinister smell! (However, some members of the family have of course been cultivated to provide useful food – carrots, parsnips and celery.)

Holly (an old name, 'hollens') is surely in the hedge. Here again the red berries suggested to the ancient herbalists that they might be used to stem bleeding; they were dried and powdered and used internally and externally. In the days when I was living so frugally that I had neither coffee nor tea, I made a useful hot brew from the young leaves of holly. The taste was stimulating, somewhere between an inferior tea and coffee. There is an affliction called by my old country doctor 'holly rash', which affects the hands and arms of countrymen – occurring around the time when holly is being harvested for the Christmas trade. Holly varies very much in its scratchiness and is related very distantly to poison ivy; hence the rash. When I was selling my holly the local buyer tried to convince me that he had to offer a lower price for the less popular and specially hard-to-handle 'porcupine holly'. If there are no berries on a holly in season, it is probably because it is a male, for male and female flowers occur on different trees.

There is invariably hawthorn (whitethorn, or May tree), usually the main constituent of a hedge where it makes an effective spiny barrier; indeed the word 'haw' has the same root as the old English word for hedge. The all-pervading fragrance of its white flowers ('May') in early summer has no match. I remember a lady telling me about the time when in a near-drowning incident she was resuscitated from the point of death. She said that she now knows what it is like to begin to die – she was in a sort of dream, drifting effortlessly down a lane overhung by sweet-scented 'May blossom'.

I was warned as a child never to pick the hawthorn flowers as bad luck would follow, and if they were taken indoors someone in the family would die. The berries (haws) are edible but, to me, tasteless. To the birds in winter they are manna, and my local red squirrels enjoy them.

The blackthorn, sometimes found in hedges where it is even more effective a barrier than the hawthorn, though less prolific, often makes a great show of white flowers before leafing in early spring. Its spines have a reputation for being poisonous and I can vouch for this to my cost, as I was once laid up for weeks with a painfully poisoned knee after collecting a spine when hedge-cutting. The small plum-like berries, the sloes, might tempt one to sample, but regret follows immediately for they have an explosive bitterness. When I shared my home with an orphan roe deer fawn I had raised, I could not suppress a shudder as I watched the animal enjoying the fruit, picking it skilfully from the hedge and ejecting the stones. The sloes of course are used to make that best of all Christmas drinks, sloe gin.

There are poisonous plants in hedges and one is the climbing black bryony, with shiny, heart-shaped leaves, indistinguished flowers but shining scarlet berries. Another also has very attractive fruits: bittersweet, or woody nightshade. It is one of the sinister *Solanaceae* family which includes the poisonous deadly nightshade, the black nightshade, the henbane, the very poisonous thorn-apple – but also the potato, the tomato and tobacco! The hedge-loving bindweed, with its attractive funnel-shaped white flowers, is also poisonous.

Ivy is in most hedges. The black fruit of ivy is also regarded as poisonous, though once it was used as an emetic, and in a louse-killing hair wash. Birds eat the fruit with apparent impunity. It is interesting that the lower leaves take on the typical ivy-leaf form, but those at the higher, flowering, level assume a more regular oval shape. This is a characteristic of the holly too. In ivy's ancient ancestry the lower leaves were prickly like the holly; higher, out of reach of animal browsing, there was no need for that defence.

Crab apples are often found in hedges. In its wild state the crab is spiny, though if it is not in this form it may have grown and reverted to the wild from a discarded core from a cultivated apple. The flowers are very attractive, pale pink buds opening to white. The fruit varies in tartness, even though to the unwary the often rosy-red colouring might suggest otherwise. Yet from ancient times crabs were eaten; 'roasted crabs' would 'hiss in the bowl' in Shakespeare's time. Nowadays it is often made into a delicious jelly. All the varieties of cultivated apples have been raised from the crab.

There are two garlics growing in the hedge foot, though they are not related. Ramsons is the familiar woodland plant with the attractive crown of white flowers, and leaves like the lily of the valley which give out a powerful scent of garlic. I remember a farmer telling me that he had to pour away the evening's milking after some visitors had left a field gate open and the cows had got amongst the ramsons. The milk was tainted. If he was geared to making cheese, he might have invented a new variety. The leaves were often used in the kitchen in older times, as were the nettle-like leaves of garlic mustard or 'Jack by the hedge' which make one of the earliest appearances in spring.

If the hedges are loaded with autumn berries, are we going to have a hard winter? This is an old wives' tale. What happens in the autumn depends upon what happened before to stimulate the flowering and subsequent fruiting of the hedgerow. It could follow a mild winter when flowers were not nipped by frost, or in the previous season when plentiful sunshine at the right time ripened the flowering wood.

WALLS AND STONE

As we walk along there may be other things to note. A ditch and bank by the roadside may be the boundary of an ancient woodland long since felled. Straight lines of hedges and walls criss-crossing the countryside may tell of the agricultural revolution and the Enclosure Acts. In areas where there are stones aplenty, fences may be of dry-stone; flora-wise they may have little to offer beyond lichens and ferns, but they are works of art. Most drystone walls (or 'dykes' in some places) are really two walls leaning on each other, filled between with 'heartings' or small stones, and locked together with occasional long stones going right through. The tops of the walls are protected by a capping of stones ('cam stones') placed either vertically or at a steep angle. The way in which they are placed is the waller's signature. I know one wall where the craftsman had a sense of humour and he chose the most grotesquely shaped stones to decorate the top. The reason why a drystone wall can stand for many years is that it can move with the land, for land – particularly on a slope – can 'creep'. A rigid cemented wall would crack and fall down.

Where walls are numerous and massive, it might be that they have been made merely to accommodate stones cleared from the agricultural land on which they stand. Ruins or heaps of stones in the landscape, sometimes a series of earth mounds, could record the violent days, or the destruction or migration of a population during plague or famine years.

The stones of the local parish church – built solidly when most contemporary houses were probably of wood or wattle and daub – have much to say, and there is a whole book of parish history in the memorials in the graveyards. I never regard graveyards as morbid places; they all have a history to tell in their stones. Note for instance the contrast between the number of children dying young, from illnesses that are no problem today, and those residents who have lived to an exceptionally late age. Sometimes the site of the church seems to be inconveniently placed to serve the settlement, but this could be because the original church was built over or by a sacred Celtic well. If the churchyard is surrounded by a circular wall, it could be that the church was placed deliberately over a pagan stone circle.

The surviving older settlement landscapes are the best. In the early times, generally from the seventeenth century, when crude houses at last became more substantial structures, the materials that were close to hand were used. The buildings blend with the landscape, for the stone was pulled out of the land on which they were built. Old villages at their best look as if they have grown out of the ground, because in a sense they have. Later, improved roads and transport brought in alien materials and the buildings sit less happily in their environs.

Searchers with eyes to see can still find the human history of earlier times as well as the surviving natural history even in ravaged landscapes. But there is yet no shortage of less damaged countryside, never too far away. It all has something to say.

10

Walking in Forest and Woodland

Nowadays one tends to think of 'forest' in the British Isles as commercial conifer spruce forests, and 'woodland' as broad-leaved deciduous woods. Since many of the forests are in the care of the Forestry Commission they offer more walking opportunities than the latter which are most probably privately owned.

For a walker there is a great deal of difference between forest and woodland, as I will explain; and no doubt my bias will show. A walk through broad-leaved woodland rewards the observant nature lover with a variety of interests.

Alas, the small remnants of the once extensive broad-leaved woodlands of Britain, including ancient ones re-established from medieval times, have been grossly deci-mated in the last decades. While, rightly, concern about the depletion of ancient forests in other parts of the world has grown, to our shame we have allowed recent accelerated destruction to add to earlier depredations in our own. Often broad-leaved woodlands have been felled and replanted with conifers. Now 62 per cent of Britain's high forest consists of alien conifers.

A typical broad-leaved woodland is an apparently random mixture of mature trees, saplings and coppice; commonly of oak, ash, beech or birch, with undercover sometimes of smaller species such as hazel, and a rich ground cover of flora. A commercial evergreen conifer forest has great blocks of single tree species in neat lines all of uniform age and height. A broad-leaved woodland changes with the seasons, from the varied shades of new green in spring to the multi-coloured glow of autumn, with the flowers, each kind blooming in its season. An evergreen conifer forest can be ever dark green, and no ground flora can survive under its unbroken canopy. A broad-leaved

94

woodland is rounded, frondose, a mixture of free and natural communities; a commercial conifer forest angular and spiky, a regimented uniformed army. Broad-leaved woodlands maintain a floor of rich soil with the decomposition of the autumn leaf fall. It has been argued that conifer monoculture produces an acid soil only fit for growing more conifers after the benefit of chemical fertilizers; and the water run-off after storms produces acidic water courses feeding rivers and lakes to the detriment of fish and animal populations.

CONIFER FOREST

Conifer forests offer more mileage for walkers in the United Kingdom since the advent of the Forestry Commission's enlightened attitude to visitors, and they have much else to offer and enjoy. Many forests now have visitor centres, and if one is available it is advisable to visit it first in order to pick up leaflets on recommended walks and tree identification.

Trees of all kinds are fascinating plants – conifers especially so, for they are among the oldest examples of land plants. They belong to the primitive order of gymnosperms, which bear their seeds 'naked', usually in cones, instead of being protected by a fruit. The oldest examples in the British Isles, dating from about 200 million years ago, have been found fossilized in coal measures. Gymnosperms followed the primitive ferns and fern-like plants and predate the advent of the flowering plants (*Angiospermae*), which include the broad-leaved trees, by about 100 million years. However, many of the early conifers became extinct, and our only native representatives now are Scots pine, yew, and juniper, which is really a shrub.

Nowadays the conifers of commercial forests are all alien species. The commonest tree favoured is the Sitka spruce, (*Picea sitchensis*), introduced from the north-west of America in the nineteenth century. In its native temperate rain forests it can grow up to 300 feet high, majestic and handsome with its silver needles. Even here, when left, it can grow to an impressive size, but it is not generally allowed to reach that stage. Often planted in large, dark blocks, it is ubiquitous. Its popularity with foresters is due to its great adaptability. It will grow rapidly almost anywhere – and it does – and can grow where no other species of tree will thrive. It provides a good harvest of wood, and is much used in pulp manufacture for paper-making. The Forestry Commission would like us to love their Sitkas, the 'super tree', and suggest that we might call it 'silver spruce' for it is going to be with us for a long time. It looks like a Christmas tree, but be not deceived; its needles are so aggressively prickly that it cannot serve that purpose comfortably.

I have very mixed feelings about Sitka. I have seen it soaring to great heights above its almost impenetrable undergrowth, in the rain forests of the north-west Pacific coast, the haunt of black bears and bald eagles – a vividly unforgettable, soul-stirring experience. But at home I have worked uncomfortably amongst its pigmy brothers. Those needles somehow manage to insinuate themselves through to underclothes and into boots! When a plantation encroaches upon a footpath, passage can be decidedly unpleasant.

If the Sitka is renamed 'silver spruce' it should never be confused with the silver firs, which are far more attractive. One of them from the western American continent is 'grand fir' (*Abies grandis*), but is more choosy of soil. In reasonable soil it can compete with Sitka in rapid growth, and can be seen in some forests. The common silver fir (*Abies alba*), an alpine species from Europe introduced into Britain in the eighteenth century, seeds naturally so well that it can be found in broad-leaved woodlands in England, Scotland and Ireland.

The softer-needled spruce, the Norway (*Picea abies*), is the popular Christmas tree recognizable by its smoother, pinkish trunk in contrast to the Sitka's scaly surface. There are still extensive Norway spruce areas, some planted exclusively for the Christmas trade.

Another extremely common tree of commercial forest is the larch, a deciduous conifer. The most attractive of all the forest conifers, it is unique among them for it sheds its needles after they have turned gold in autumn, and it becomes fresh green in spring, with tiny red flowers. Mixed among the evergreens, it makes a pleasing contrast. While the earth beneath the dark canopy of Sitka is generally devoid of plant life, at least in the spring light can reach the floor beneath the yet needle-less larch, and some grass and plant life can survive. European larch (*Larix decidua*), from the Alps, is so resinous and rot-resistant that it can be used as fence-post material without treatment by preservatives. However, since the European is subject to disease a quicker-growing Japanese larch, and a hybrid from the two, are now more usually grown.

The British Forestry Commission is bound to favour fast-growing conifers like Sitka and we have to accept them. What is to me, and to most naturalists, *not* acceptable is the clear felling of broad-leaved woodlands to be replaced by the faster-growing, more commercially profitable blocks of conifer.

The Commission was set up after the First World War to grow timber and reduce reliance on imports; that was the sole purpose. But since the 1960s it has been recognized that the forests are an important recreational resource for the public. Once, public access was discouraged for fear of fire; nowadays it is recognized that visitors to the forest can act as observers, and if a fire does occur the alarm can be quickly raised.

In recent decades the Commission has shown some commendable dedication to conservation. Some of their forests have areas of broad-leaved trees, and more are being planted. In some, healthy deer populations are maintained, and some even have hides available from which the public (on application) can observe the animals. Nesting boxes are sometimes erected too. The rare pine marten and the polecat live unmolested in Commission forests and there is no persecution of the predators as there can be in some privately owned forests, where gamekeepers are employed to supply a crop of game birds.

Aesthetics are now also a consideration. In new planting

policies the harsh straight lines of the forest boundaries which block off chunks of hillsides are being broken up to show a more natural thinning and curving of the edges.

Although we may deplore the mathematically laid-out, enslaved lines of conifers, and the fact that they are an immigrant population, we can still relate to them. They are not lifeless blocks of wood; they are brethren in the web of life that embraces us all. The molecules that give them life are basically, in their fundamental chemistry, the same that give substance to ours. Forests of all kinds complement our lives, for they absorb our waste gas, carbon dioxide, and breathe out oxygen, without which we – with all mammals – could not survive.

PLEASURES AND PROBLEMS

A conifer forest can have much to offer the walker. For one thing, it gives the opportunity of escape from other people. On a busy day in the country walkers on the hillside are revealed, and a sought-for sense of remoteness might be elusive. A forest can swallow greater numbers, yet create an illusion of solitude. Walking out into an open hillside is one experience; the enjoyment is in the open prospect, extroverted, a sense of freedom. A walk into a forest brings a more intimate, introverted, experience: a different kind of escape – a more cosy, wrap-round freedom.

The episodes of surprise are near at each turn in a winding forest track. Some would add that a clean, resinous scent in the air brings a feeling of well-being. The forest offers shade in the heat of summer, and shelter in bad weather.

The other things on offer are more subtle. We can enjoy the effect of light in the forest: its filtering through the open areas; shafts of light breaking through a canopy in a morning mist; filtered light like that from stained glass. The sound of wind in conifers is the restful, soothing sound of the sea. In a felled area a conference of foxgloves, shoulder to shoulder; pure magic this, the dormant plants having seized the opportunity that they have awaited for years. There are mosses, fungi and lichens; the latter almost luminescent in contrast to the dark trunks and branches of their anchorage. Deer tracks are to be seen in soft ground. The indignant sound of the ubiquitous wren can be heard.

On this green stage we can include the human actors; forest workers, clad like space-men in their protective gear (hell on a hot day!), sawing, felling, manoeuvring logs with heavy precision machinery. The pleasing smell of new-cut wood can be enjoyed. Everyone who is at leisure likes to watch other people work, and as long as watchers do not get into danger they are usually welcome.

Bird flocks come into the conifers. Favourites of mine are the goldcrests, our smallest birds, busying about the boughs, the air full of their fairy-like piping. If there is more incisive chatter, busy acrobatic movements and a shower of cone fragments, there are the strangest and most exciting of the conifer denizens, the colourful crossbills.

If the terrain on which the conifer forest is planted is interesting – rock outcrops, some water – and if the Commission has cut viewpoints, or allowed them to remain open, even planting broad-leaved trees around them; and when they have taken the trouble to excavate ponds, and opened up the dense canopy in places to encourage a diversity of wild life – then we should applaud their efforts in supplying some very interesting and worth-while walks. Walk routes for public use in some forests have been specially engineered.

One is almost compelled however to take a leaflet and follow the forest's recommended routes. It is almost inevitable that the large-scale map one might have is out of date as far as the commercial forest is concerned, for forest roads are continually being made, some areas are clear felled, new areas planted. Even the forests' own maps can be out of date. What must be understood too is that forest roads do not necessarily lead anywhere in particular! They are extraction routes winding around the forest along which the harvested timber is removed, and they often finish at a 'banjo', a loading area and vehicle turning place. What can considerably complicate map-reading is where forest roads have been driven along rights of way. The walker is led along confidently, then at some point the forest road diverts; the unsuspecting walker continues on the road, unaware that the route of the right of way has been abandoned. Indeed, where the true route leaves the forest road the forestry bulldozer has probably left a large obscuring bank!

Although one might be free, subject to forestry operations, to walk where one likes, it is not normally possible when lost to get out of trouble by walking on a compass bearing. Close planting, brashings (stripped branches) on the forest floor, low branches etc. are almost impossible impediments and the compass can only help in a limited way to overcome confusion. Forestry plantations can produce a crisis of confidence in a very experienced map-reader, and reduce the strongest to something verging on a nervous breakdown.

The forestry organized routes are usually graded to suit all walkers and are waymarked. If this is well done, it is hardly possible to go wrong. However, in my experience the information given on mileage and time taken should be treated with reservations! In one Scottish forest I know, I think the suggested walk times were worked out by an Olympic runner. And one thing which the leaflets do not usually warn against is the summer-time attention from flies; a fly-repellent should be in the walker's tool-kit!

Some may think me churlish for being critical when I have enjoyed so many days in the forests of England, Scotland and Wales; but I do think that the Commission should more fully accept the importance of public access and give more attention to its needs. Walkers are warned that they could be disappointed in one or more of the following ways:

(1) Footpaths churned up by timber extraction to a sea of mud. This is inevitable in the short term, but too often the paths are not reinstated for months or even longer.

(2) Paths left almost impassable by piles of brashings.

(3) Notices such as 'Path closed owing to timber operations' left in place long, long after the timber operations have finished – maybe a year!

(4) Nature trails poorly organized and not maintained.

(5) Direction notices and waymarks removed during timber operations and not replaced.

(6) And, hopefully less common but by no means unknown, public paths blocked by new planting (Commission's explanation: 'It is easier working practice to plant solidly and clear the path later'); and footpaths blocked by fencing and waiting for stiles.

All this might seem puzzling when every forester one meets, even the contractors whose presence is often ephemeral, are usually friendly and helpful. Trouble-free routes depend on how much that individual forest is committed to accepting public recreation, and whether there is a ranger on the staff with the authority to see that the necessary tasks are done.

It should not be assumed that all conifer forests in the British Isles are owned by statutory authorities. Many of them are in private hands and access through them may be restricted to public rights of way and highways, if any. Some forest owners make a charge for entry, which of course is reasonable enough if the routes offered are private; the paths have to be maintained. However, it would be a sad day if government proposals to privatize the Forestry Commission's holdings are realized without a commitment to free public access.

The maze of forest roads can confuse a sense of direction. Lacking landmarks, even the foresters themselves can miss their way. One winter evening, a veteran worker at a forest's office asked me which way I was going. When I mentioned a village over the other side of the forest, he asked if I could give him a lift and said he would direct me on a short cut on forest tracks rather than by going round by the public road. I agreed. It was fast gathering dusk when we set off and the winding way through the darkening spruces and track junctions was complicated. After thinking for a while that the route was farther than I expected, I stopped the Landrover and suggested that we might have come in a circle; I recognized a crooked larch in the headlights. 'Nay,' he said, 'carry on as I tell you.' Some time later I stopped again at the same spot and he uttered a forest oath. 'Aye, you're right! Me reckonin's out. And I've worked 'ere most of me life! Just keep goin' straight and we'll get out someways!' We did eventually. I seldom go into a conifer forest without the latest forest map, and never without a compass.

WOODLAND

Walking in a broad-leaved woodland or forest is a completely different experience from walking in a man-made commercial conifer forest. There may still be the confusion of forest tracks that were made for timber extraction and lead nowhere in particular, but the similarity ends there – utterly.

You are walking into what is a supreme natural interdependent, self-perpetuating communion of living plants and animals in its myriad forms. There is tremendous variety in the scene, and it is dynamic. There are the changing seasons. Walk in summer the same woodland which you walked in winter, and it will be unrecognizable. The winter woods are wide open, there are distant prospects. After spring brings to it a green mist of leaf bud and bird-song, summer's curtains of full leaf close in the scene. Each few steps one walks becomes a different scenic episode, the closing and crowding of visual experience giving an illusion that the woodland is far larger than it is.

Spring brings its many subtle shades of green, its tree blossoms, and a wealth of flowers: commonly the first – the prima rosa – primrose; and the dainty woodland daffodil, shy violets, the white stars of wood anemone. And bluebells! No other European country can boast that blue which carpets our moist woodlands – a colour that changes hue according to the time of day; a dense and dark blue sea when the sun is low, powder-blue at other times. It is hardly possible to capture the colour on film. In one magical wood I know the blue shades out into the milk-white of stitchwort, and is splashed with the red of campion. The scent is almost too much.

Then summer days can be heavy with the pungent smell of ramsons – wild garlic. Some may not like it, but to me it suggests health and cleanliness! Everywhere, even sometimes growing on the moss of tree boles, there is wood sorrel. Chew the clover-like leaves for a refreshing tang! And there are others that invade the glades: yellow stars of celandine, and the smaller pimpernel, and St John's wort; purple ground ivy, blue bugle, rose-coloured valerian, the several purple orchids, the pink of herb robert, later the tall spires of digitalis – the foxglove in communities; the wild rose; that rich evening scent of honeysuckle! And the many more plants in their chosen, special habitats. Clumps and colonies of ferns in variety, and the many mosses, complete the picture. If one can walk quickly through a winter wood it is hardly possible in summer, for there is so much to detain the observing walker.

Woodland too has its moods – that exhilaration of birdsong in early summer's dawn chorus; the brooding, healing, utter silence of a winter's day; the soft and serious conspiring conversation of trees as they move in the wind.

Perhaps first it is necessary to clarify the difference between a woodland of 'standards', and 'coppice' woodlands. In managing woodlands, trees can be allowed to grow on to a good size and then felled for timber. The spruce of a commercial forest, a soft wood, grows relatively fast. By comparison a broad-leaved tree, which is a hardwood, grows slowly; it might take half a century or more to reach useful maturity. This fact did not bother the woodland owners of old, who planted for their grandchildren. Nowadays there is a different commercial philosophy – enjoy a quick return; the grandchildren can look after themselves.

The quicker and more profitable option in broad-leaved woodlands, used everywhere up until this century, and almost from time immemorial, was coppicing. In this system trees are felled in winter, and provided that grazing animals are excluded from the woodland, a number of shoots spring up from the stumps ('stools'). These grow on to provide strong, broad stems, which can be cut at a useful thickness at twelve- to fifteen-year intervals. A coppice then is woodland with most of the trees consisting of a number of stems or trunks growing from each stool. Only broad-leaved trees can be coppiced.

There was an enormous variety of uses for the coppiced timber: arrows, spears, and bows; spoons, cups and bowls; the making of charcoal for smelting metals; clog soles and chairs; walking-sticks, hay rakes and besoms; tool-handles and hurdles; hoops and baskets; wheel-spokes and ladders; cricket bats and tennis-rackets; fences, and gates; rollers and rolling-pins; and countless others. No household could be without a product of the coppiced woodland.

Nowadays, although there have been recent revivals in the coppice industry here and on the Continent, coppicing is not regarded as offering a quick and lucrative return. Alas, many of the skills have been lost and need to be relearned.

Sometimes woodlands are managed as 'coppice with standards', where selected trees are allowed to grow on to maturity to produce sizable timber, amongst those that are coppiced.

What could confuse is that a woodland could be named on a map as a coppice (say 'Smith's Coppice') when it is no such thing, the name having outlived its description. It might be that at some time long past the coppice system was abandoned and the stems 'singled'; that is cleared out, to leave only single trunks ('standards') to grow on to mature trees. Or very likely the coppice has been clear felled and replanted with conifers!

COMMON SPECIES

To get the best out of a woodland walk it is first necessary to be able to identify at least the eight common woodland tree species which can be standards or, in six of them, coppice. It is relatively simple to pick this up when the trees are in leaf and you have the help of a book.

The oaks are easy, for the leaves are so distinctive in the three commonest species. It has always been the most valued tree. To the ancient Celts it was revered, and the first temples were sacred groves of oak. Oak timber is unrivalled for strength and durability, and oak woods have been cultivated and cropped and coppiced since early human settlement. Throughout history oak woods were a vital part of the rural economy; they provided 'pannage' for swine – a feast of acorns – and the cropped and coppiced timber had a hundred uses, from making bowls and furniture to building construction, and in ship-building. Even the bark of oak was used – it was boiled to provide tanning for the leather industry. Oak is home for a vast number of insects, and consequently a feeding ground for the many birds. As a fuel, when dry it burns hot and slowly.

Ash should be easy, too; typically growing tall and straight, racing rapidly upwards for the light (the species is well named 'excelsior') with clean light grey 'ashen' trunks, the older trees developing rugged furrows. The leaves are 'pinnate' – the narrow-toothed leaflets arranged opposite each other along a single stem – and are some of the last to appear in spring from jet-black buds. After the oak, the ash has always been the most useful tree for timber; it is very strong, straight-grained and adaptable. Quick to coppice, it makes the best tool-handles; and of old, weapon handles, lances and spears, and bills. In fact, ash timber fits every bill; it was extensively employed as framework in wagons, coaches, and formerly in the motor industry. The fine wood was in such universal demand that it was once exported from Britain. Even the ash seed 'keys' were once used – boiled and pickled in vinegar as a relish!

In Norse mythology an ash tree, Yggdrasill, linked and sheltered the nine worlds. From an ash tree the first man was created, Odin breathing into it the spirit of life. Yggdrasill is often a feature in Norse stone carvings on tombs and monuments.

Often ash is happier growing in limestone areas, and in limestone uplands it can survive very hostile elements, though of course not growing to great size; but in 'acid' soil woodlands it thrives often in ravines and where spring water has 'flushed' minerals to the soil surface. A great survivor of damage, it can continue in life even if quite hollow. It burns well, even when green.

Beech woods are common; the smooth dark grey trunks and the dense cover of papery bright green leaves are a give-away, plus the fact that the canopy is so dense that there are hardly any other trees in competition, and few plants on the brown leaf-covered floor. However, beech woods glow a bright pale green in spring, and are a glory of vivid reds and browns in autumn. Beech is the third most useful timber tree, as it is straight and fine grained and it has always been used to make furniture. In commercial beech woods the trees were usually grown on to maturity and felled at their best when a century old or more, the space left quickly regenerating from seedlings. In years when the beeches produce a good harvest of seed ('mast'), it is raided by flocks of birds. Bramblings join the finches, and where roads run through beech woods and car wheels break the shells of the fallen mast, many other bird species feed on the kernels.

People seem to find the birches more difficult to identify. They will not often be found in numbers in dense woodland, unless the woodland is pure birch, as the trees are light demanders. They are the 'pioneer' trees that begin the formation of natural woodland, colonizing waste ground, quarries and crags, as they first colonized the land long, long ago after the retreat of the Ice Age, forming birch woodlands until invaded by other species. The loosely applied name 'silver birch' is something of a misnomer. The bark is generally white and black, papery smooth, though rough at the base, the twigs smooth brown. Saplings often have a shiny, reddish bark. The leaves are a pointed oval, with the edges toothed. The wood is not much favoured by foresters, being too light and susceptible to insect attack and rot. But birch is so prolific, even in hostile environments, that it has long been an all-purpose wood, particularly in highland areas. It is easily coppiced and grows quickly. Even the twigs were – and still are – used to make besoms. The redolent bark was used in tannery, and of old the sweet spring sap was fermented to make ale! Birch burns quickly and hot.

The floors of birch woods produce a variety of interesting

fungi, including the outrageously red caps of fly agaric (pixie stools!). On the trunks of the trees the 'razor strop' (*Polyporus betulinus*), a bracket fungi, grows. Problem – does this tough rubbery fungi kill the tree, or does it only grow on dying trees? Birch trees are not particularly long-lived anyway.

Sycamore should be easy to recognize. It is one of the maple family, with the typical five-lobed leaf. The bark is smooth grey, though scaly in old age. It is not a native tree, but was introduced from the hills of central Europe long ago. It so readily seeds successfully that it can often take over a wood if allowed. The white, tight-grained wood is used in furniture making, and has special properties valued for the making of the sides and backs of violins.

When cutting sycamore in late winter, I have always been surprised at the amount of sap flow from the stump. Could it be boiled to produce a syrup like its maple cousin?

Holly needs no description. Pure holly woods are unknown, but there is hardly any broad-leaved woodland without hollies, seeding where birds or squirrels have carried and fed on the berry harvest. Holly does not grow into a large timber tree, but the hard white wood has long been favoured by wood carvers. As a fuel, it burns best of all.

Scots pine (originally and very commonly 'Scots fir') is our only native pine. Although of course it is not a broad-leaved tree, it is included here because it can occur naturally in broad-leaved woodlands. The pine was once the major tree in the wantonly destroyed Caledonian forest – the vast Scottish pine forest which probably covered about 6,000 square miles. Now its sad remnants – about 50 square miles – are mainly in reserves, some areas so thinly spread that they could hardly be termed 'forest' at all.

With its very ancient ancestry, the Scots pine is another pioneer tree which followed the birch in colonizing the land after the last Ice Age. It spreads rapidly in peaty or sandy soil anywhere once established and undisturbed, and defies the storms on exposed upland, adapting its shape to the prevailing wind. The resinous wood had many uses, not least through the centuries for lighting homes. Thin strips were cut from the heartwood, dried, and burned in iron holders to light the rural cottages. Torches were made from the roots. The needles are dark green; the trunk though is a distinctive feature, being a warm rufous colour and flaky. In its youth it has the spire shape of a fir, but later – given space – it develops an individual and attractive, and to me very expressive, broken crown.

This is a really superb tree. To see and smell the pine woods in their natural highland habitat is a rare treat. There is nothing quite like it; they fit so perfectly in a wild environment. To walk amongst them on soft needles with the cones crackling underfoot is my idea of a happy experience.

Pine of course, as other conifers, cannot be coppiced. Scots pine has been planted with other introduced pines in commercial forestry, but not now to any great extent. Grown in close ranks in a forest it loses much individuality, growing tall and slim with a characterless crown.

Yew too, our native evergreen, is a conifer, not producing seed in a cone but held in a bright red fleshy cup. Very distinct with its dense mass of glossy dark green needles, it is less common in woodlands, although it is a natural woodland tree. In some instances yews have grown so densely that they have stifled competition and now form pure yew woods under which there is perpetual twilight. To walk then amongst their red trunks, footsteps silenced by the carpet of needles, is a unique and moving experience. One might feel the need to talk, if talk one must, in whispers.

Individually the yew is often seen growing in churchyards, where it can be easily identified. It was planted there as a symbol of everlasting life – it is evergreen and can live on for many centuries. Some of our churchyard yews are very ancient indeed; the trunks of old yews are often massive, reddish-brown, the bark peeling in thin flakes. Yews are very tenacious, and can live on growing massively for hundreds of years even after the trunk has become quite hollow. As every woodman knows to his cost, the wood is extremely hard; almost metallic. It has played its part in history, for yew was used to make bows for the bowmen of old and no other wood would do. The timber is extremely durable, and furniture made from it has great value as much for this as for its beauty – its red heartwood contrasting with the white outer wood. It has often been planted as a hedge, and used in topiary.

The few other specifically woodland trees include the wych elm, which has the general features of the field elm, or small-leaved elm which grew massively in Ireland and the English lowlands before being struck by Dutch elm disease. It coppices well. Small-leaved lime is another natural woodland tree, but scarcer, and its presence can mean that the woodland has ancient origins.

No space is wasted in a broad-leaved woodland. Wherever there is enough light filtering downwards there is frequently an 'understorey' of shrubs, and the hazel is often the most common, seldom growing above 15 feet (4.5m) high. There are usually several stems rising from one stool, for hazel was – and still is in some places – coppiced to provide stakes and sticks. Its growth is quite rapid. Leaves are a pointed oval, and are downy. It displays the delightful catkins, or 'lambs' tails', in spring when the tiny red female flowers are often overlooked. In autumn it produces the famous nuts, beloved by red squirrels, jays (the noisy woodland bird), and country-goers. However, I am now very reluctant to take the nuts as that would be robbing the red squirrels which are losing much of their natural habitat.

Learn to recognize these few trees, and that is a start. The rest must come with observation, for trees which are not particularly woodland species usually have a corner somewhere. Alder and willows for instance will occupy wet areas, and gean – wild cherry – crab apples and poplars might occupy their chosen places. Sweet chestnut (not to be confused with horse chestnut, which is not a woodland tree) has been planted in some woodlands to provide coppice wood for chestnut paling, poles and chair-legs.

NATURAL HISTORY

Once the woodland tree species are recognized, any observant person can see that each individual tree is unique in the way it has grown and adapted itself to fit its particular niche in the woodland scene. To me, a tree has always been a source of wonder. The shape of any individual tree has not been determined in the embryo within the seed. Once the root reaches down, and the tender shoot and seed-leaves begin to absorb the sunlight, it must respond wholly to its place in its environment. It reaches upwards to the life- giving light as its roots explore the earth for minerals and water, and for anchorage. If the light is too restricted, the growth of a tree is slow; though once a neighbour falls, making a gap in the canopy above to reveal the sky, it will race for it. The direction the expanding trunk takes, and the number of branches it pushes out to any side to capture light, are determined by the light's availability. It must also take account of the prevailing wind, and its height and vigour is affected by the depth of the soil and the root competition from neighbouring trees. Every tree tells its life story, which is there to be read if we only take time to move around it and study it. Each tree is as obviously individual as each human being. The outstanding characters amongst them – the rugged, the majestic, the crooked – can be easily appreciated and recognized. This means that once one is familiar with a woodland area as a community of unique companions, one is less likely to get lost!

On the matter of getting lost, an oft-repeated 'fact' needs killing – or at least qualifying. It is said that you hardly need a compass in woodland, for everyone knows that 'moss grows on the north side of a tree'. In fact, the type of mosses which grow on trees need sustained dampness and cannot survive direct sunlight. In the heart of a woodland hardly any direct sunlight reaches the damp base of a tree, so moss can be growing on all sides; whereas a single tree standing alone in an unshaded field *will* have moss growing mainly on its northern side. A better direction indicator is the way tree crowns are shaped by the prevailing wind, but even this needs qualifying. If the wood is sheltered from the region's prevailing wind, the winds may come from a modified direction. Here again it is far better to rely on one's map-reading skill.

A mixed broad-leaved woodland is a naturalist's treasure house. In the supremely balanced community of plants, animals and birds, each species occupies its allotted place. The woodpeckers can illustrate the way that habitats are shared. The green woodpecker or yaffle, which has that distinct mocking laugh, feeds low and often on the ground, raiding ant-hills; the greater spotted woodpecker feeds from tree branches, while the lesser spotted lives high in the tree crowns.

There is no better way to observe and enjoy woodlands than by finding a comfortable place, sitting down quietly and patiently, opening awareness and letting it come to you. Typically you might hear a slight noise in the leaf carpet before you; watch the spot, and an ever-hungry foraging shrew could emerge, moving in quick little spurts as if its engine is misfiring! At their active time of day in summer birds are numerous: resident chaffinches, robins, tits and wrens being joined by the chiffchaff, willow, wood and garden warblers, blackcaps, whitethroat and lesser white-throats, and spotted flycatchers. One strange little favourite is the tree-creeper, defying gravity as it scrambles up the tree trunks and around the branches. At night, the tawny owl makes his patrols.

The woodland animals can only be seen by quiet observers, and that means placing the feet carefully when walking and keeping conversation, if any, to a whisper. The wood floor is occupied by the wood mice and bank voles which are hunted by the fox, who also eats many beetles, though a rabbit or a pheasant would suit him better. Foxes are only encountered by chance, though once one can recognize their distinct scent their near or recent presence can be detected. Grey squirrels are common in many woods; the more attractive and shyer red squirrel is resident in more isolated areas in Wales, northern England, Scotland and Ireland. Their populations rise and fall for no obvious reasons. Weasels and stoats, and in some places the

111

rarer polecats and pine martens, also occupy the woods. Badgers have survived terrible persecution very well in many parts of the British Isles, but being nocturnal and normally extremely cautious, they are seldom seen and their exceptionally keen nose warns them of possible danger. The only certain way to see them is by joining a naturalists' society group which organizes badger watches in small parties.

Several species of bats occupy any hollow trees, and one can sometimes see them flying in daylight. I have watched with fascination a Daubenton's bat, for instance, coursing a mill pond, flicking flies off the surface.

Where there are known to be deer in the area dogs should be on a lead, otherwise they may take off on a scent and could be lost for hours. Deer are at their most active at dawn and dusk, and can normally be seen in daylight only by accident when approached downwind from them quietly. Their hearing and scent senses are keener than their eyesight. The commonest wild deer, and to my mind the most beautiful of our wild animals, is the small roe deer, commoner indeed than one might suppose as they are very cautious and move away at the slightest hint of an approach. The largest of our wild animals, the red deer, is normally only thought of as occupying the heather moors and highlands, but in fact in these circumstances it has adapted itself to that environment. Its natural home is in open broad-leaved woodland. A woodland stag is better fed than its moorland brothers, and is much heavier. The sight of a gloriously majestic woodland stag defending his harem at rutting time, with his magnificent mane, and his antler spread, sometimes deliberately festooned with bracken to make himself more impressive, is one of the most memorable experiences the countryside can offer.

I suppose that I am biased, for my formative years were spent working in the woods. I can enjoy the stark reality of the mountains, the freedom of the moors, but I cannot be long away from trees and be happy. A wood is cool in summer and a shelter in winter. A woodland area is a perfectly balanced self-adjusting environment. Left to itself, free of man's domestic grazing and browsing animals, it is self-perpetuating. As a tree dies of old age, and falls, it leaves a gap in the canopy and tree seedlings seize their chance on the woodland floor which is suddenly full of flowers. The dead tree provides a rich environment for fungi and crumbles to enrich the soil. Wherever one stands only part of the woodland's living pattern can be seen. If we move quietly through it on a walk, we can hardly fail to feel that restful atmosphere, that harmony, a symmetry that appeals so much to the human soul . . . Every walker should walk a woodland. But tread carefully, for woodlands are very special places.

11
By the Sea

Land life is confined to one quarter of the earth's surface, so in effect we are all islanders. Sooner or later most of us make for the margins of the sea. The sea is the beginning, where all life had its origins; sea water contains all the elements needed by living organisms. When the first mammals were able to abandon reliance on saturated oxygen from the sea and adapt their gills to take gaseous oxygen from the air, they could crawl out on to dry land, but must perforce take the life-sustaining sea with them wrapped in their water-proof skins. Every dry land animals carries its allotted sea and humans are no exception. We taste the sea salt in our sweat and our blood. The sea flows through our veins, most of our body weight is nothing but salt water.

If the sea is in our bodies it also occupies part of our inner self and our instincts, for it has always been vital to human existence. The earliest human inhabitants of the British Isles came by the sea, built their settlements by the shore and lived largely from its harvest. Since then the lives of generations have been enriched from the enterprise of those forefathers who have dared to ride the seas. Every one of us must have seamen ancestors.

Perhaps at holiday times the attraction for many of the sea and the sun is a touch of nostalgia that haunts us all? Maybe to experience it helps to fulfil a spiritual need of which we are only vaguely aware?

If one is to get away from the man-made scene to the natural, the seascape has an enormous advantage. There can only be minimal human interference with a seascape – no intrusive edifices of bricks and mortar, no concrete or macadam. And if there is an oil rig out there in the bay, it is dwarfed by the wide expanse. The unrelieved picture of sea and sky may lack variety; on a long voyage even the sighting of another ship may be greeted with exaggerated relief. But the sea is very rarely still. There is much to absorb our attention when we walk where the sea breaks on the shore. Merely the restful rhythmic sound of it can be balm to the soul. And when it is a hot, windless day inland, a cooler breeze from the sea can often be enjoyed as it replaces the hot air rising from the land.

But to those of us who find lounging in deck-chairs boring, the beaches offer some good walking with plenty of interest. Most of the miles of sea beaches around the British Isles are available to the public provided that there is access to them along rights of way. Exceptionally, some limited areas of beaches have been closed off quite legally by landowners. The foreshore though – that is the land between high and low tides – is generally open to access and it is a navigable area; if one can boat over it at high tide, one can walk over it at low.

From a natural history point of view this area is a unique habitat, for it is inhabited by life forms that cannot be found anywhere else. This is its fascination; it is a teeming, thriving world of its own.

TIDES
Obviously, before setting off on an exploration it is necessary to know when the beach will be exposed. The outgoing spring tide exposes the most beach – 'spring' here having nothing to do with the season. A spring tide occurs when the moon is new, or full. It is at these times that the gravities of the sun and moon are pulling approximately on a straight line; the sea is pulled furthest up the beach, but also goes furthest out. The opposite is the neap tide; after the spring tide, the effect of the pull of the moon and sun gradually decreases as their positions relative to the earth change; the sea advances and retreats for a lesser distance up the beach until in seven days the minimal movement of the neap is reached. Then the distances gradually increase for seven days until the next spring tide. The spring tides gradually reach their highest on the approach of the

equinoxes in March and September, when the sun and moon are in a straight line.

So before exploring the beach, walkers should find out the time of high tide. Tide tables should be available at seaside towns and villages; though the table is of course only a guide, for the information is based on a certain datum point. Tide time and height may differ at some distance away. For instance, the tide will reach a promontory sooner than a bay. Tide tables would be less necessary if high and low water were always at the same times, but unfortunately they occur around fifty minutes later each day. Ideally the walk should start as the sea retreats from high tide, and one should aim to get back well before it recurs, unless there is a return shore-line walk above tide level.

If the walk is wholly on the beach, its length is determined by the time of the next high tide. Watches should be checked so that one knows when the half-way point of the walk is reached, and it is necessary to start the return journey to beat the tide. *This is important*. It is easy to underestimate distance in the level landscape; you may have enthusiastically walked farther than you think, particularly if the beach is firm sand.

LIVING THINGS

On a rocky beach anyone deeply interested in living things will not walk far without finding something to enjoy. There is so much to see. First, there is the great variety of seaweeds. As a very general rule there are three types, depending upon the amount of light that they need. The green weeds utilize the maximum light nearest the shore; they are often in hair-like or moss-like mats and slippery to walk on if footwear is unsuitable. Farther out, and frequently left stranded on the beach after storms, are the brown weeds, notably the wracks – bladder wrack and egg wrack – which need less light. In sheltered bays there are often waving forests of brown oar weeds which just break the surface at low tide. Farther out still are the more delicate and attractive red seaweeds which utilize light from the blue spectrum which penetrates farthest into deep water.

Every rock pool is a little world with its forest and lawns of seaweed; what may be found is dependent on the amount of exposure or shelter. It might seem a bizarre world where animals like sea anemones and sea cucumbers look like plants, and other animals move sideways. Impossible things happen where life flows so vigorously. For instance if an animal loses a limb, or even its vital organs, it can grow them anew. Each pool has its special collection of sea urchins, fish, prawns, starfish and crabs. Loose rocks can be turned over to see the creatures living beneath (the rock must be replaced afterwards to preserve them). The variety of life is so great that if one was to try to identify everything a wheelbarrow full of books would be needed. It is best to take with you a general guide on sea-shore life. The shells are relatively easy to identify with the aid of a good book, and their varied forms and colours are fascinating.

The other attraction of the beach walk is beachcombing along the strand line where the tide has left its jetsam. Alas, nowadays there could be a lot of very nasty plastic, but treasures can still be found, though the much-sought glass trawler net floats are now rarities.

A pebble beach may not be so rich in life, but the wet pebbles themselves can shine like jewels. Every single one is unique. Any exceptionally attractive specimens, too good to leave, may seem to lack lustre when dry; but taken home, a coat of clear varnish can bring out their beauty. One can see, and better still pick up and feel, the difference between those pebbles formed from sedimentary rock, which are worn flat and saucer-shaped, and the other extreme of harder and heavier plutonic rocks which are globular. On some shores it is possible also to find fossils.

Wave power can be appreciated and enjoyed from a safe viewpoint above an exposed rocky shore at high tide. I swear there are few more restful occupations than sitting over a rocky inlet watching successive waves pound in, retreating and colliding, creaming round obstructions, trying to climb the rock, sucking back, thrashing and roaring, hissing, snorting and spouting up fissures, throwing up a rain of spray. One can indulge in the absorbing guessing game of predicting each big surge, and the height of the collision between advance and retreat.

On a rough day, wave power can be devastating. Great boulders, concrete sea defence blocks, can be lifted like corks. This is no time to be anywhere near a beach, and hardly a time to be walking above the shore; though an octogenarian living by the sea once told me that one of the secrets of his good health was that he always liked to be out on the coastal cliffs filling his lungs 'with pure oxygen' during 'a good blow'. It certainly does one good occasionally, wherever, to share the passion of the wind; it invigorates the body and clears the mind.

Some of the most enjoyable walks are along the coastal footpaths. There are superb sections in the Pembrokeshire Coast National Park which are ablaze with flowers in early June. There are miles of walking along the Somerset and North Devon Coast Path, and on the Cornish granite cliffs. Some too in the North Yorks Moors, and there are sections all around the British Isles. This is great walking in clean air, with sometimes ancient castles and forts, and old-world fishing and smuggling villages for variety.

The flora of the coastal fringe has to withstand salt spray. Salt will not allow the common inland weeds to grow, so the flowers are specialized. The finest flower of the cliffs and rocks is the popular sea pink, or thrift, which blushes at its best in June, but flowers on into September. Bindweed is a menacing weed inland, but the carpets of sea bindweed with striped pink flowers are a joy. Sea holly is a special favourite; it glows blue and is sometimes shamefully removed by flower arrangers. Pink salt wort and sea pea, mauve sea aster and sea lavender, white sea campion and mayweed, and the early flowering scurvy grass – which used to be chewed by seamen to ward off scurvy – and the startling yellow of the horned poppy, are only a few that can be enjoyed. The varied colours of the coastal rocks also owe much to their embellishment of the reds, orange-coloured, greens and greys of the lichens.

BIRD-WATCHING

The coast is always an area favoured by bird-watchers, and even if you cannot put a name to many of the sea birds, the gulls being tiresomely difficult, you can still enjoy watching their effortless flight, hardly flapping their wings but taking advantage of the lift from the coastal up-currents of air. The kittiwake is an exception to the common gulls, for it can dive underwater for its food. But the great spectacular sea bird which I always enjoy watching off the northern coasts is the gannet. A large bird with black tips to its white wings, it can see fish below the sea's surface, make its calculation, climb to a height where its dive can take it to their depth, and then make that spectacular drop from as high as a hundred feet, folding its wings a fraction of a second before it hits the water. To see a flight of them flashing in the sunlight, plunging in the water together, is an unforgettable spectacle. I have walked amongst them on their great nesting site on Bass Rock in the Firth of Forth, and I swear that they are the most handsome of sea birds, yellow-headed with a touch of green on the cheek, and black brows that make them look stern and knowingly intelligent.

Other sea birds are more easily identifiable. There are the dainty small terns, great gliders, long-winged for their size, and with a forked tail. There are the auks. Everyone can recognize the small, chubby, clown-like red-beaked puffin; they nest in rabbit holes on the cliff-tops. The guillemot is another of the auks, head and back black, with a white front; it nests on cliff faces, as does the razor bill which looks similar but has a heavier beak.

The sometimes black-looking mysterious bird, standing on rocky islets with its wings spread out like a heraldic figure, is the cormorant. An ungainly, large primaeval-like creature with a snake-like neck and a long beak, it flies low, with slow wing beats, and swims low in the water, but it is the great underwater hunter. Its smaller cousin is the shag; I have happy memories of seeing them sitting in rows on rocks on the Irish coast.

Viewpoints over mud flats and salt marsh are for the dedicated bird-watchers, for the species seen include the many waders, ducks and geese. These are magic places. Here one can hear the unmistakable bubbling call of the curlews, the plaintive cry of the oyster-catchers, the sharp pipe of the sandpipers. Some of the salt marshes are nature reserves, havens for wintering wild fowl and geese when they are at their best time for a visit.

But to me the most evocative of all sea-side sounds in spring is the exclamatory cooing of the eider duck – a questioning, phantom sound haunting the morning mist.

The sea calls. We cannot delay a visit for long.

12

By Waterside Paths

An enjoyable walk for me, with landscape changes all the way, would be one following the passage of the hill stream into the river, and along the river bank.

FROM STREAM TO RIVER

Let me trace it by imagination. I start high on the hill in low, wet cloud. Mist and rain drifts in from its origin in the sea, and in its marriage with the rocks and earth of the hill, the stream is conceived. Here below a crag, at a patch of bright green reached by a scramble, is the womb. There are flowers here, flora of woodland and meadow, incongruously in this otherwise exposed place, for water gradually draining through a great depth of rocks and welling up from below has brought with it minerals it has leached in its passage.

From here I follow a trickle of water as it descends the hill. I walk on wet hummocky ground by a channel curving through the rocks, which becomes deeper as more water oozes in through moss, liverworts and golden saxifrage on the channel sides. As I descend, the growing volume of water is at last audible as it chuckles over stone obstructions. Further down the light increases, and suddenly I am out of the cloud. I walk over many tributaries. At last it is a stream banked by rushes and ferns; it knows where it is going and makes its way purposefully and more noisily over falls and spillways, until as it flows quietly through peat bog I pick the firmest way through sweet gale, the bog myrtle. My steps stir up the delicious aromatic aseptic scent – that quintessential fragrance of wild places that I sometimes dream of when I am an urban prisoner. There is nothing quite like it. Once, sweet gale was used to make ale; it must have been nectareous.

The bog is a gathering ground for all the water taken from the valley head. I am stepping over a family of streams one by one, and the main course now has grown to such a force that it has cut down through the foot or two of peat to a base of clay, rock and stones, and it widens as it reaches a flood plain.

Here there is a cheerful clamour of noise as the water ripples over a bed of many water-worn stones. To describe the sound is impossible, for it has many parts as each of the hundreds of impediments to the boisterous flow produces its own sound. A chuckle somewhere, a babbling elsewhere, rustles and gurgles and chattering, purlings and tinklings, rattlings here, sputtering and bubbling there. Hundreds of insistent voices sounding off all at once like a crowd at a market.

To the sight it is all greens and greys, glints and sparkles, white and cream, dazzling and flickering, gleaming and glistening and glittering as each swirl and ripple, and each exposed wet and polished stone, reacts to light. It is a wonderful, cheerful place to be.

But at last, on reaching a grove of alders and willows, the stream joins another and, according to the map, is officially a river. The mood is now completely different – pensive, speculative, for the water is deep enough to run almost silently over its smooth-stone bed, talking to itself in only a mere murmur as it sweeps the mossy banks. After the cacophony this is almost a relief. It seems to flow without fuss, down to its green depths; it looks heavy and sluggish until a leaf sweeps by, and then I know it flows fast.

RIVERSIDE

The map shows a riverside path below a narrow road at the far side of the river. I follow an unmarked anglers' path around the knotted roots of alder clumps until I reach a farm track and a stone bridge which I noted on the map.

One can never cross a bridge without leaning on the parapet to watch the depths, where the bridge's shadow has cut out the reflection of the sky. Staring long enough, it is possible to make out the fish, hanging incredibly nose to current with hardly a movement of tail or fin. A miraculous thing is a fish; it has matched its flow of life to the flow of the river. Unlike clumsy land animals, it is obviously and quintessentially at one with its element.

Once the first fish is spotted others can be seen, and one wonders why they were missed before. Should I be joined by a companion it is practically impossible to point out where the fish are; he must stare long enough to spot them for himself.

Across the bridge the riverside path meanders on the bank round the grotesquely shaped clumps of coppiced alder trees like old witches turned into wood, picking out the firmer ground. The marsh marigolds between the path and the river have long since finished blooming, but the yellow iris – 'flags' – stand like companies of soldiers; a brave show. There are the peculiar 3-feet-high camel humps of tussock sedge. Understandably, these large natural cushions were once cut to provide hassocks for the church.

On a viewpoint mound, I survey the river for one of my favourite birds whose pretty confusion of liquid notes I have just heard. The dipper is there as he or his companions always are – a compact little brown and chestnut busybody with white chest, standing on a round stone in midstream. He bows several times, then performs his amazing feat – he dives and disappears into the swift current to cling to stones on the river bed hunting for insect larvae and small molluscs. When he rises the current takes him a short way until, fluttering little wings in the water for a while, he takes flight back to starting point.

Downstream the water deepens as it falls over a shelf and swirls round rock islands. It is purposeful, but I have seen it in other moods: after drought, a noisy trickle of itself; in a hard winter, its shallows covered in ice and snow; in heavy flood, angry, obscuring the riverside paths, the fall a roar, sweeping by with a burden of floating debris. I have even seen it once in such a spate that, with a noise over general pandemonium like artillery fire, it bounced boulders along as if they were rubber balls.

Now between the river and the path is a display of riverside flora – more notably tall reeds; and a show of pink great willow-herb among the cream foam flowers of the so voluptuously scented meadow-sweet. Here and there lie patches of beautiful purple loosestrife and pink hemp agrimony. Then where the path closes to the river on to an obvious rock platform viewpoint, smoothed by ancient floods and used by anglers, I sit and enjoy watching the movement of the river across to its wooded opposite bank. It moves variously, in mid-stream gleaming with reflections of the sky, by the banks darker with the moving reflections of the trees. Here near the bank, where crooked tree roots are swept by the water, there is a swirl which has trapped green leaves which turn incessantly. Farther out the water has heaped itself over half-buried boulders with troughs on their downstream side, a source of much of the river's deeply sonorous music. This has stirred eddies, which mysteriously constantly change position. From the green water in mid-stream a fish leaps up through the ripples. On the far side a low alder branch touches the current and swings constantly like a metronome.

I am soothed by the sound and if I sit long enough my feelings are one with the flow of the flood. Why is river watching so addictive? The river has meaning; like an old, familiar tale told it has its beginning and end. The flow is older than the earliest human visitors. How many generations have stood on this bank? In the river's time their brief moments have come and gone like fleeting shadows.

The river's flow is like the flow of time itself, insistent and unceasing, and this may be a clue to our fascination, for here we can watch it go by; the past leaves us downstream. Upstream pouring towards us, is the future. Time flows on and, godlike, we are mere fascinated spectators. We are not involved.

The passing irresistible flood may remind us that time has nothing to do with clocks and watches, mere measurers pretending to catch moments. Time does not stop at each minute and hour, no matter how razor-sharp a micro-chip may try to define them. There is no dividing line between past and future, they are one. It is impossible to define the present time. There is no now for, as we point to it, it has already slipped by, down-stream, into the past . . .

Further, as I progress, the flow power of part of the river has been channelled between stone slabs. Here there is the remnant of an iron and wooden sluice through and over which the water now pours noisily. This was a mill-stream which turned a great wheel, now no more, and I must make my way to the narrow road for here is a hamlet which once had a hard working water-mill, now a house. The hamlet is off the major road routes, and if there is time the pub is worth a visit, for there is a welcome and, thankfully, it is one of those hostelries that are getting rarer: it has not yet been tarted up to provide for the motor trade!

There is the little church which *was*, alas, tarted up by a Victorian benefactor, but still rewards a visit. Under yew trees lies a little churchyard. Not so many very old stones here, for the ground was not consecrated until two centuries ago, and before then corpses had to be carried out of the valley to a village 6 miles away. On the low hills on both sides of the river, half hidden by trees, hedges and stone walls, is a scattering of cottages with their gardens. By the road-side with lawns going down to the river, a fine Georgian house stands beyond a huge old sycamore. There is a little barn-like chapel, and the one local farm where once there were four. The river flows through all, an asset and a blessing which was one good reason for the settlement's beginning.

Beyond the hamlet lie the ivy-covered ruins of another mill, and I can leave the road to pick up a riverside track. Below another fall the river's pace slows down and spreads wider and silently as it meets reed-covered levels. This was anciently a small lake, but has long since been filled with silt and colonized by willows and birch. It is rather soggy going and I must pick my way carefully, crushing aromatic water mint, and watch out, for in places the water has undercut the bank that I am walking on. There are sweeps of yellow water lilies now in the river to delight the eye, and small neon-blue dragonflies everywhere. Along the bank side I

125

must make my way among reeds and rushes, and in the water's side there are stands of reedmace (commonly called, erroneously, bulrush) with their surprising brown clubs, like cigars, which are really the female flowers below the ephemeral fluffy male flowers.

By the path-side I look for purple marsh orchids, and as always here I am not disappointed. They are plump and healthy. Growing singly, they are easily overlooked. Here too there are clumps of fine yellow globe flowers, the most handsome of the buttercup family. The area is a-buzz with insects. A large grey dragonfly flits past, the click of its wings quite audible as it switches direction. Then there is a delightful blue-green iridescent damsel fly; I have just begun to delight at its passage, by the river's flow, and then I notice several more close all around me – and more beyond. They are everywhere. One perches briefly on my sleeve. The river and the riverside are their whole world. Magical creatures of a short season – a brief enough time to us; a whole long-stretching life-time to them.

After this flat area the river narrows as it passes through a stony area again, the remnants of a moraine, a natural dam, that was once the end of a glacier. There is a modest cascade, a good place to picnic by, and then the water flows through banks of willow flanked by lush farm pasture. I pick up another anglers' path, for this is a good area for fishing. Once otters were common, taking eels mainly; now they are only occasionally visitors. I have seen kingfishers here, and sitting quite still I have observed the most spectacularly coloured bird for minutes at a time, fishing from his perch on an alder stump.

I rejoin the road at another bridge. The walk must end here, but the river runs on through farm fields and a market town to an estuary; and to its end in the everlasting sea which gave it birth.

CANALS

Such is a riverside walk, though most river banks are only accessible in snatches. If you would walk by water, albeit still, canal banks have more lengths of path to offer. The towpaths are not necessarily rights of way, though miles of them can be; and if they are not, walkers may be allowed by reason of long custom. The flora of the river banks have their counterparts by the canals. Indeed in some ways there is more variety, presumably because canal traffic has carried seed from far distance. There is the advantage of long levels which should attract the less athletic walkers. And one can wonder at the skill and ingenuity of the engineers, contractors and navvies who planned, dug, burrowed, and constructed the waterways, and revolutionized transport from the eighteenth century until the coming of the railways.

LAKES

One waterside walking area remains: by the shore of freshwater lake – which would include mere, tarn, loch, lochan, llyn, or lough. It is fortunate if there are paths making the circumnavigation of the lake possible. To attempt a walk otherwise (unless possibly the water is low, allowing walking on exposed beach) could usually mean fording streams and rivers, and getting involved in bog where one could get inextricably glued, as well as doing environmental damage. Normally we might have to be content to reach a limited footway on a piece of lake-side access.

A lake in a hill area, devoid of excessive human impact, offers a perfect landscape, with the heaving shapes of the background balanced by the placid levels of the water. A fine landscape's general appreciative impact might be hard to explain. It is immediate, it is harmony; and is to the eye what music is to the ear. It is 'yang and yin'; the male and female elements; the active and the passive; a happy meeting of contrasts. It demands more than a brief glance. It is surely this apparent conciliation between the two displays of natural forms which can suggest restfulness. If we have time to stay and enjoy what we see, it might even encourage us to come to terms with our own inner conflicts.

So the attraction of the relatively still water of a lake is quite different from that of sea and river. It is restful and quiet. On a still day on the bank there is only a gentle lapping, maybe a subdued whispering in the reeds. On a very still day even this is muted as the water almost imperceptibly rises and falls as if the lake is taking breath.

I will allow that there are other, rarer days when a wind, funnelling through the surrounding hills and spinning angrily as a result of their obstructions, can whip up the water into a turmoil of white crests. It can sometimes pick up the surface to cause water spouts which tear across the lake like demented white banshees.

The lake-shore flora matches that by the riversides, but the still shallows are home to other plants. There is the bogbean or buckbean with its delightful fluffy white and pink flowers. There may be expanses of yellow water lilies, but also the exotic white which opens only in sunshine, the most beautiful of all the wild flowers. It has a drawback, though; if picking is attempted for a display its scent is rather vulgar, unlike the yellow which smells vaguely of brandy! In Wales, Ireland, Scotland and the north of England one might find the delicate pale lilac-coloured water lobelia.

The lake too is the place for bird-watchers, at any time when birds have their presence. There is the ubiquitous coot, the small black swimming bird with the white forehead (hence 'bald as a coot'?). Its explosive 'kik-kowk' is one of the lake's evocative sounds. Less gregarious, the similarly dark-coloured moorhen haunts the lake-side reeds and is often found feeding amongst vegetation at some distance from the lake.

Among the other birds around the lake one can maybe see mallard, the common duck world-wide, the male unmistakable with his showy green head and purple breast, contrasting with his rather drab brown mate. There should be a heron around if it could be spotted standing still among the reeds, and there may be resident mute swans. The great crested grebe may be present – that comical-looking water bird with ear tufts and long chestnut cheek feathers – and a visit in the spring can reward us with the strange mating display, when the pairs swim together swiftly breast to breast with cheek ruffs extended, contorting their slim necks up and down in unison.

Little grebes, goosanders, reed buntings, snipe, tufted ducks and goldeneye are among the others which may be seen and heard around a lake, and swallows and swifts may be skimming the water. But come winter a cocoon of warm clothing, a flask of something, a bird book, a pair of binoculars and a well-favoured lake, or a reservoir, could yield surprises.

Lake scenery is of course where the landscape photographer and the artist come into their own. But every lake has its moods. The artist, the photographer, the connoisseur put on boots and rucksack early, for the lake's still beauty is shortly after morning's first light.

Ideally that is the time to enjoy all natural landscape. Our minds should be clear then, undisturbed by dreams of the night, and free from the concerns of the day.

13

On Moor and Mountain

Some walking enthusiasts may suggest that ordinary low-level country walking is for novices; and that all walkers ought to graduate to the nobler and more demanding art: from the more or less horizontal to the slightly more perpendicular.

They will say that the ultimate adventure is only in the high places. Are you to be persuaded? What is it about the heights – moorland, fell or mountain – that has this strange hold on so many people?

There are a number of reasons why people are drawn to the hills, and having much to do with feelings they can hardly be rationalized. Their spaciousness encourages an *extreme* sense of freedom; a refreshing relief from the feeling of being confined; from the demands of everyday life a temporary escape which could hardly be more remote. That is a special kind of freedom – that dares to escape completely the reminders of the man-made trappings that cushion our lives. Some might call it an expansion of the soul. If one has never tasted the delights, the reaching out, the adventure, sometimes the discomfort, way up above the human anthills of normal existence, it is impossible to understand. The ultimate experience could be walking a ridge wrapped around with nothing but sky.

It can be a journey into sanity, back to bare basics. As Byron wrote:

> I live not in myself, but I become
> Portion of that around me; and to me
> High mountains are a feeling, but the hum
> Of human cities torture.

To some it is a test of oneself, a challenge and a satisfying sense of achievement. I remember seeing the glow in the face of a young man on crutches who had made the top of one of the Langdale Pikes, heaven knows how. Fitter men may climb to the roof of the world, but he had climbed his Everest.

If the climb for some though is *only* an ego-boosting device, it loses my sympathy. Our mountains should not be looked on merely as massive open-air sports stadiums.

Another motive is that urge to explore; to go into the unknown; to see what is on the other side of that hill. It is that strange compelling motive which has spread humanity throughout the globe. If I try to analyse the source of supreme enjoyment I have experienced on one of my happiest climbs, not at all the highest – that lone scramble over the snow-covered pinnacles of Aonach Eagach sheer above Glencoe perhaps – I could only say that the feeling is beyond the telling: it was that strange, tingling exhilarating mixture of everything that we call adventure.

A caution: any novice approaching moor or mountain climbing should be warned to disregard the show-offs who are met with at every hill resort. One should pay small attention to the person who always seems to be around, who asks where you have been, and who will tell you that you ought to go higher and farther. Some may suggest that you have not really lived until you have cut steps in ice to reach some savage alpine peak. Some may say that mountain walking is fine . . . but it is a tame experience unless it involves some severe rock climbing. If you do something that has stretched muscles and endeavour to the utmost, and then arrive back triumphantly at the inn, there will doubtless be someone who will say that he did your route at the age of twelve and that he has just done something twice as hairy and the following day will do something even greater!

Do not be tempted by these characters to do more than you really want to do. Be wary too of the person who offers to lead you on a hill walk; he could be an idiot seeking an ego-trip.

I believe that if we are to learn anything at all about living it is vital to understand that ultimately no one but ourselves

131

can decide how far, or how high, we want or *need* to go in any of life's endeavours. How far or how high anyone wants to *walk* should be determined by experiment and experience; it is entirely a matter of personal choice.

It is a fallacy to believe that the higher the better, for it is not only the height of the experience that counts – but also the depth. It is the *depth* of the experience of which memories are made.

A modest hill could do. Indeed it is possible to enjoy a lifetime of walking without ever putting foot upwards on a serious climb. If adventure is defined as an encounter with any novel or unexpected event, then that experience can be relished in any country walk.

If the second definition of adventure is preferred – an enterprise involving elements of uncertainty, hazard and risk – yes, then the hills offer their challenge. It does not follow however that the greater the hazard and the greater the risk – whether real or imagined – the greater the adventure. In my own experience the enjoyment of an expedition can be marred by fear, and an excessive flow of adrenalin! The pleasurable feeling from the experience then is almost entirely in the luxury of retrospect, whether immediate or much later!

It is hardly possible to go through life without meeting extreme danger at some time or other. This is an important part of human experience which, like the prospects of a hanging, concentrates the mind no end. But only the irresponsible *seek* danger. Risks are fine as long as they are calculated risks. I am all for adventure in the sense of the second definition. If that is what you want and hill-walking is the answer, the question is how much common sense should be mustered? Too much would inhibit any excitement. Too little can lead to disaster.

The big mistake is to believe that walking on the high hills, the moors and the mountains is just a more strenuous form of country walking. It is not. It requires not only a good standard of fitness but, as my grandad would say, a bit more 'application'.

MOUNTAIN WEAR

Hill, moorland, fell, mountain, what is the difference? Very difficult to define – best to think of them as all one.

To begin with it is necessary to apply one's thoughts much more to clothing and equipment. First – the footwear. Many accidents on the hills are still caused by inadequate footwear, even though nowadays there is such a large choice available with every shopping precinct having its country sports emporium. Back in the sixties and seventies the mountain-rescue teams were getting very tired of collecting people off the heights with broken limbs from falls caused by poor footwear. Carrying a stretcher is a back-breaking task and personally, like other rescue-team members, sometimes I had to try hard to be sympathetic to a casualty I was helping to carry who had ventured into rough country in smooth-soled town shoes. It grieved me, and my colleagues, to see such hopefuls struggling up the fell paths convinced that they were taking no great risks. It is one thing to climb upwards in poor footwear – coming downhill is quite another matter. *95 per cent of falls happen on the way down.* On the ascent, toes can be used to dig in and bear the body weight. Footwear has to become a braking system on the descent, and smooth soles and heels are useless, especially so in the wet or on dried-out grass, when they might as well be made of banana skins.

Obviously hill paths are bound to be rough. Their surface has to endure extremes of fierce hill weather, the soil is usually poor, and the vegetation (if any) is thin and cannot easily endure human and animal tread. So one is often walking on bare stone, amongst cobbles or boulders, or in deep and messy peat troughs, often on testing slippery steepness, sometimes on loose and unstable scree. Footwear must be adequate to all this, as indicated in Chapter 2. It has to hold firm around the ankles, the uppers have to put up with knocks and cuts. The treads on the soles and heels have to be stout and they must remain so. When they get too worn down, they must be retired or re-soled.

Where the going is particularly messy or wet, it is an

advantage to wear gaiters above the boots to prevent nasty egress through boot-tops and to protect the legs.

As conditions in high places are notoriously changeable, clothing must be robust and windproof. The original jeans made of sailcloth may have been windproof and serviceable, but normal fashion cotton jeans are useless. Not only does the wind blow straight through them but they offer other hazards. Once on a rain-swept day on the fells I saw a young lady approaching me and walking very oddly, stiff-legged, rather like the bride of Frankenstein. She was wearing new jeans which had shrunk skin tight in the wet! Her companions had to all but carry her downhill.

A glance back at the records through the years of mountain accidents shows that on wet days in midsummer months there have been tragic deaths from hypothermia – all from inadequate clothing. I remember particularly one wet July day in the Lake District mountains when two young men who were racing, trying to beat a time record for ascents, both died. They were wearing only cotton singlets and shorts.

The most dangerous weather of all is heavy rain driven by strong winds. Without shell protection and warm clothing beneath, it is deadly. The coldness is increased by the wind chill factor. In Snowdonia, the Lake District, and in the Scottish and Irish mountains, this 'Atlantic' weather can come suddenly in summer. A rescue team could be out on one day attending to someone suffering from heat-stroke; and the next picking up someone who has collapsed from hypothermia . . .

The outer clothing – an anorak – should be totally windproof. It could be waterproof too, though totally impervious wear, as has been said, induces perspiration. If the outer is not waterproof, then a separate waterproof should be carried. The carrying of proofed over-trousers is also necessary. Some recommend brightly coloured clothing so that one can quickly be seen in an emergency, but as I have said, many like myself hate the sight of bright red, yellow or orange figures littering the mountain landscape. It can ruin the impression of wildness.

The adequate windproof clothing for the day, which should include a hat, needs to be supplemented with spare clothing in case conditions get worse. The rucksack should always carry (with the all-over waterproofs) at least an extra sweater, and gloves.

EQUIPMENT

Some of the other items to be carried need to be considered. Food should be light-weight and nourishing. All hill-walkers have their favourite choices and sandwiches are the obvious. Sardines eaten straight from the tin were once much favoured. Bread spread generously with jam (this becomes a sticky mess) is an old favourite, but many swear by it. I used to prefer bread spread with honey and sultanas. In fact dried fruit – perhaps apricots and raisins – is a good addition to stem the pangs of hunger. There should be a flask of tea, coffee, or soup. It's not a good idea to carry a bottled drink – too heavy. (As a general rule water from a mountain stream, sited above any habitation, is fit to drink. However over-indulgence, particularly if the water is very cold, can cause the dreaded 'belly-warch'. On hot days the water can be better used as a refreshing mouthwash.)

In addition there must be those iron rations which are saved for emergency only. The recommendation should be for something that produces energy fast – containing sugar or glucose. The classic item for the mountains is Kendal Mint Cake, which has been carried to all mountain areas in the world and eaten on Everest. I am never without it. Some prefer to carry a tube of sweet condensed milk, but this can be indescribably messy if it bursts! Others prefer to carry something that they would not normally like to eat, so that they can resist the temptation to pretend an emergency!

The first-aid kit should be rather larger than that carried for ordinary walking; it should include at least one larger wound dressing, and some triangular bandages (*see* Appendix 3). One must read up on first-aid beforehand too. Read particularly about the symptoms and treatment of hypothermia; about resuscitation, and the need to put casualties in the 'recovery position'. In all but midsummer time a light-weight torch should be included, in case of a delay meaning that you are overcome by darkness. Obviously a reliable watch is necessary; a pocket-knife is often useful; a whistle should be handy for an emergency. (Six blasts on a whistle, or six light flashes repeated at intervals, is the internationally known mountain distress signal.)

A large brightly-coloured polythene bag (a 'survival bag') does not weigh much, and should also be in the rucksack. It can be a life-saver. One night when in snow on a mountain rescue I shared one for several hours with my German Shepherd search dog. It was not exactly three-star accommodation and I cannot say that I slept much, particularly as the dog woke me at regular intervals to make sure that I was alive and to assure me that he was very much so. The bag's usefulness is that if one encounters a casualty he can be put in the bag out of the wind and weather until the mountain-rescue team arrives. The reflective plastic 'survival blanket' one sees on sale, and sometimes used at the finish of sporting events, is useless for the windy conditions on the hills.

It goes without saying that good large-scale maps are essential and that prior to setting out the hill-walker has gained some essential skills in map-reading. The map should always be kept handy, not buried in the depths of the rucksack. The obligatory compass is ideally one of that modern type with a transparent bowl marked off in 360 degrees, set into a transparent plate. The popular ones are the Swedish 'Sylva' or the Finnish 'Suonto'.

PLANNING A HILL WALK

Good planning is essential and in any party one person must be the acknowledged leader. The route should be determined beforehand, with the least able member of the party in mind, and it must have possible 'escape routes' in case a walk has to be abandoned for bad weather, twisted ankles, fading muscle power or some other unforeseen event. It is a very good idea to study a reliable guide book first to see if the route is feasible.

There should also be a 'Plan B' in case the weather forecast means that the main 'Plan A' must be discarded. *This is vital.* So many rescues involve parties whose plan is so rigid that they *must* reach their summit regardless of the bad weather. One can understand the bad feeling this causes to rescue teams and police who know that casualties – perhaps exposure or avalanche victims – have foolishly braved conditions that would deter local shepherds and very experienced mountaineers.

The other major planning fault is to be over-ambitious. It is folly to plan a long route unless one has worked up to it. On a mountain-walking holiday the first day or two should be 'limbering up' times on short easy routes.

Mountaineers use variations of the old 'Naismith's rule' (touched on in chapter 5) in planning an expedition. The basic formula is to plan to do 3 miles (4km) per hour, and to examine the contours and add one hour for the ascent of each 1,500 feet (460m). This safe formula can be adjusted up or down after practice; but it is prudent to err on the safe side, more particularly in strange territory. To the walking time one should add break times for refreshments, photography, contemplation etc., and a 'fail-safe' addition for any other eventualities. The best plan, having worked out the time for the walk to finish (*at least a half hour before sunset* at the outside, or sooner) is then to calculate backwards to make sure that the start time is correct. A map route-measuring wheel can be obtained from most outdoor sports shops, and takes out some of the distance guesswork.

Having decided upon the plan it is a very good idea to write it down and leave a copy of it with someone at 'base', wherever that may be – just in case of accident so that the rescuers have some idea where to find you. In mountain areas some hotels, guest houses and hostels have special record forms for this purpose.

Look at the contours seriously when planning an off-the-paths route in open country. The shortest distance between two points on a map is not necessarily the easiest and quickest way. If possible one must avoid losing height only to have to gain it again, even if this means considerably

137

lengthening the walk. Remember that contours close together mean steepness, and avoid having to negotiate areas shown with the 'crag' symbols on the map.

The last planning job is to check the local weather forecast (*see* Appendix 4). If poor weather is forecast, then go to 'Plan B'. There is little point in reaching the heights if they are to be obscured by thick cloud. It is amazing too how vastly different the exposed summit can be from the lower slopes. Poor weather in the valley could mean appalling weather on the heights. This is particularly so in spring when the daffodils may be in bloom in the woods, but stark winter will not have left the tops until late May, or even later.

SETTING OFF

Start the walk coolly dressed on the assumption that the first upward steps will bring a warm-up. And do not start at a rush; go slowly to allow the muscles and oxygen-feeding lungs to get tuned up.

It may soon be realized that the path shown clearly on the map is not so clear on the ground! Or there may be several paths on the ground instead of just the one marked. 'Sheep trods' are easily mistaken for footpaths and can lead one well astray. This is where map-reading is so critical. *No one should venture on the heights until they are experienced map-readers*. The map should be handy and easily referred to. Some prefer to carry it in a transparent plastic case which can be slung on a cord around the neck. Tardiness leads to mistakes. Sometimes, particularly in a high wind when the map blows about every which-way, or if finger-ends are cold, it is tempting to leave the map in a pocket and guess the route. Foolish! Fingerless mittens keep hands warm and make map handling comfortable. Of course one has to put up with the unwritten laws which decree that any given critical point on a map is on a crease; and that on reaching an awkward problem on the ground and opening the map wide, it is suddenly hit by a force 10 gale; that is what makes hill-walking so interesting!

138

Hill-walkers should know how to use a compass effectively; this was dealt with in Chapter 6.

SAFETY RULES

There are some basic safety rules for hill-walkers. The first one is: never be afraid of turning back, no matter how disappointing the decision might be. The party leader must make that decision, and everyone should comply without argument. The experienced mountaineer knows when it is necessary to abandon the main route plan; it is the novice who ploughs on regardless.

The leader should *never* allow his party to become split. Time and time again rescue teams are turned out to look for a person missing from a party. Typically, one member of a party complains to the leader that he/she is not able to continue the climb. That person is told to stay put and wait for the rest, who will do the ascent and pick up him/her on the descent. Often the leader has underestimated the ascent time and the individual, tired of waiting, possibly feeling cold, unwanted and demoralized, wanders off. Or sometimes the leader has a mistaken idea of where the person was left and completely by-passes the place on the descent. The victim of this incompetence is usually the weakest member of the party and this situation is very serious if the weather is poor. It has led to sad fatalities.

Another not uncommon situation is when a member of a party complains that he/she is unable to continue and is told to return to the valley by the way by which they have just come. The member, very possibly without a map or the ability to use one, makes an error and goes off route and into danger. If a party member *has* to be sent back to the valley, possibly feeling unwell, he or she must *not* go alone.

One less common but potentially very dangerous situation on even our lower hills is the onset of a thunderstorm. If a storm approaches it is prudent to get off a prominent height and sit down in a crouched position away from rock outcrops or stone walls until the storm has passed.

Beware of fording streams/becks/burns or rivers. They can offer extreme danger and routes should avoid crossings

139

as much as possible. I once – and *only* once – made the mistake of assuming that a burn in the Scottish Highlands, a mere thread on the map, would be as crossable at some point as a Lake District beck can be. The burn was about 4 feet deep and a frustrating 15 feet wide. We had to make a detour of miles after searching in vain for the shallows which one can expect to see at a wide point. Once when an expected footbridge was washed out I was only able to cross the torrent at another point by using a broken spar of the bridge structure as a 'third leg' on my upstream side.

Never assume that one mountain area is like another. For instance, if hill experience is gained in the Brecon Beacons, it would be necessary to re-learn all over again in tackling the more rugged and broken terrain in the mountains of Snowdonia, the Lakes, or in the Scottish Highlands.

Beware of deep bogs. After one or two encounters they should be easily recognized! The surface of the worst is flat and usually a much lighter, lusher green than the surrounding terrain. Some have a 'crust' of what appears to be stable ground. If the ground trembles underfoot – beware! There is bog below! Some bogs are little more than a nuisance, but there are others that are deep and dangerous. It is some help to remember that heather or bracken does not grow on very boggy ground.

I recommend the avoidance of scree runs too. Scree – a steep shoot of loose stones – can make a rapid descent from a mountain possible. As the scree moves underfoot, it is rather like descending a downward escalator. However – particularly if they have been very regularly used by hill-walkers – they are potentially very dangerous. In places the scree might have moved from bedrock, leaving a smooth surface thinly covered with detritus and very slippery. Another hazard is being hit by rolling boulders. Some of the outdoor pursuits centres have wisely banned scree descents.

In early summer snow can remain a hazard to walkers on mountains in the British Isles. It can last until May and sometimes in places, particularly in the Highlands of Scotland, beyond. Out of the winter period it is usually wet with the consistency of half-cooked rice pudding. Best to avoid it.

In winter, snow is a hazard to people who normally enjoy their walking at lower levels. It is a bonus however to the experienced hill-walker equipped with the winter tools: ice-axe and crampons. Winter mountaineering in snow and ice is a specialized activity and it needs special skills. It is more serious mountaineering, and is beyond the scope of a book on country walking. All that needs to be said is that no one should venture on to steep snow and ice until they have at least become practiced in the use of an ice-axe in cutting steps and, more importantly, in using it as a brake in the event of a slide. Courses in winter mountaineering are organized by various educational and outdoor pursuits centres, and anyone who is keen to try the sport should seek one. The Ranger service in the Lake District National Park runs day courses in the use of an ice-axe – snow conditions allowing.

Hill-walking in winter away from ice can otherwise be exhilarating. With a keen, cold wind the view clarity is far superior to what it can be normally at other times of year. One needs to keep an eye open to avoid ice, though. Obviously clothing, and spare clothing, needs careful thought. Warm underwear is necessary, with long johns (or if they are not owned, pyjama trousers do as well). It is also necessary to reiterate how desperately important it is to consult the weather forecast, and to remember to check the time of sunset, and to be down in the valley *well before it is due*. That means giving the estimated walking time in the planning stage plenty of slack. To be benighted in summer is bad enough but in winter it can be fatal. Just in case – that torch is a vital item of emergency equipment!

Know the alpine distress signal: six blasts on a whistle repeated at intervals, or six flashes of light. Or the international SOS: three short signals, three long, and three short again. The reply is three blasts; but never give a reply to a distress signal until you know exactly where the signal comes from. Needless to say whistles and flashing torches should only be used in emergency.

141

No one should venture on the hill alone unless he or she has had a good deal of experience. Any single person who is keen on trying hill- or mountain-walking should profitably book a week or a fortnight with Ramblers' Association Holidays, the Holiday Fellowship (H.F.) or the Country-wide Holidays Association (C.H.A.). There are mountain-walking courses available organized by statutory authorities and by private concerns. Examine the brochures carefully! Some may be aimed at walkers with some experience, and may be too advanced. Rambling clubs invariably have some hill-walking in their programmes.

The Country Code is just as relevant on the hills as in the valleys. The hills are more often than not sheep pastures, and dogs should be under control. Left litter is particularly obnoxious. An important point on child behaviour: stones should not be thrown down hillsides or, worse still, boulders rolled. It might be assumed that there is no one below, but a party could be there though out of sight. Stone hits are a frequent cause of accidents, sometimes fatalities. If a stone or boulder is dislodged accidentally it is necessary, at once, to call out in a loud voice 'Below!' as a warning to anyone who might be beneath.

MOUNTAIN RESCUE

Every hill and mountain area in the British Isles has its rescue teams – mainly volunteers, if not all. In emergency the local rescue team is called out by a phone call to the *police* – 999 in the UK. The police are responsible for initiating rescue. If there is to be a long delay in reaching base with which one cannot communicate, the police should be told to prevent a call out. Time and time again rescue teams are turned out at night in bad weather to search for a missing party which is not missing at all but, having found itself in the wrong place, has got some nice warm beds in another hostelry without informing anyone at the place where it *should* be. This might seem so incredibly stupid that it cannot be true, but it happens time and time again! After flogging about dangerously in the darkness and rain looking for such people, the anger and frustration endured by the rescue teams is indescribable.

If one comes across a casualty, there are several things to be done at once. Give the necessary first aid, paying particular attention to breathing. The casualty must then be made safe. Move him if he is in a hazardous position *only* if you are sure that he has not got a back injury. Otherwise secure him there, perhaps by packing rucksacks around him. Place him in on his side in the first-aid 'recovery position', for an unconscious person can choke to death if he is placed on his back. Keep him warm, passing spare clothing under him as well as on top. Put him in a survival bag if necessary and possible. An accurate locality – a map reference – of the casualty must be worked out. Then someone must be sent down the hill, urged to go with care, with that information (written, do not rely on memory) and the condition of the casualty, to telephone the *police* for rescue. If there are a few people about, send more than one down for help. Stay with the casualty until help arrives.

SUMMARY

Fit people who desire to experience the nearest we have in the British Isles to wilderness should think of making for the high places, but they should be aware that the 'wilderness' experience might be spoiled by crowds. If expeditions are made in the holiday seasons, be prepared to see many others with the same intent in the popular places. To instance only some: on Dartmoor, Brecon Beacons, Snowdon (particularly the popular 'pyg track'); in the Peak District, particularly on the Pennine Way stretches; in the Lake District on Helvellyn, the Langdale and Borrowdale fells; in Glencoe in the Highlands and on Ben Nevis.

It is too easy for one long involved in mountain rescue to over-emphasize the dangers of hill-walking. I hope that I am not guilty. Any reasonably fit person of any age or either sex, skilled in map-reading, with the right equipment and with a modicum of common sense, can enjoy the freedom of the hills. The trick is to keep within one's capabilities.

It is hardly possible to go country walking without

encountering hills, but no country walker should feel compelled to ascend the mountains. Mountaineering cannot appeal to everyone. It has always made me feel uneasy to see parties of young people being more or less compelled to climb the heights in the pursuit of 'character training'. Many might be grateful for the experience, but the feeling is not universal. We see other reluctant heroes on the heights – adults sent by their employers to learn initiative and the art of leadership. I am not the only purist. Mountains are very precious places. Many feel like I do that they should be enjoyed and respected for what they are, not used as a training facility for people who do not appreciate them and will never climb a mountain again. Nor do I feel that they should be venues for mass competitive events. Fell races have their followers but I am not among them.

One can lift up one's eyes to those high hills without feeling it necessary to lift up one's feet. One can enjoy the Highlands without climbing the high lands. The great John Ruskin said that 'mountains are the beginning and the end of all natural scenery'. But he was no great mountaineer. Content to just look at mountains, he spent the last twenty-eight years of his life admiring the prospect of the Coniston Old Man range . . . from the comfort of his lake-side home and garden walks.

14

Backpacking

Most of us, way at the back of the mind, are haunted by uneasy worries about the future. Even if we are fortunate enough to have the necessities of life, we have an obsessive desire to own more and more of what are really luxuries. Yet if we are to feel secure there is one obvious truth. *Security does not depend upon how much we have; but how much we can do without.*

I would define backpacking, in the enjoyment of the countryside, as the art of obtaining the maximum with the minimum. It is the art of living well, while doing without. They used to call it hike-camping in my younger days, but the Americanism has caught on. Backpacking is walking with the basic life-support system: with a tent, provisions and cooking utensils on your back; and over-nighting en route. It is *not* 'roughing it'; it is the rejection of needless luxuries, and a return to a very simple life. It can be a learning experience – a grasp of essentials, a growth of self confidence.

I must say at once that it is not for everyone, but for the ultimate countryside experience there is nothing like it. It is as close as one can get to the natural world. There is nothing so utterly delicious as the pure unconfined, unimpeded air that comes in with the dawn to enrich your lungs. There is no green like the greenness that greets you as you slip open the tent-flaps. No jewels are as bright as the dewdrops illuminated by the dawn's break. No music is more enchanting than the sound of a dawn chorus – while you sit in the choir stalls. No taste is like a breakfast prepared for yourself in the open air. And the backpacker can go to places which are beyond the reach of the day walker.

All right – it rains. It can rain hard and long. It blows. The ground is rocky, or muddy. Some could not endure the thought of a close meeting with 'creepy-crawlies'. And you have to have ace equipment, and more than normal competence to deal with anything which comes. To some of us it is worth all that; overcoming the occasional difficulties is part of the enjoyment. Philosophically enduring days and nights of rain, and then coming up smiling gives you strength to face any other trials of life with confidence! Most readers may want to take my word for it and leave it at that, but for those who wish to go beyond simple country walking, some notes here may be helpful and are not too irrelevant to all.

First of all you must be fit. You have to be concerned about the weight you carry to the point of obsession. Every single item of equipment has to be selected for its weight as much as its effectiveness. For instance, I never carry a full bar of soap or a full tube of toothpaste. My only concession to what some might suggest is luxury is a book or two; and I have a small battery-operated electric shaver.

Now to the backpacker tent. My own – a wedge-shaped ridge, roomy for one but tight for two – weighs out at 2,050 grams. It has a nylon 'fly' sheet, outer tent, and an inner cotton tent, with alloy poles and pegs. It is made so that the fly sheet can be erected quickly first, then the tent can be hung in shelter below it – a handy arrangement if it is raining. I would never contemplate acquiring a single-skin tent.

I cannot presume to recommend a specific tent. Any purchaser is best advised to have a look at what is on offer, and to see how it is erected, asking oneself 'could I do this in the dark, or in rain?' Sometimes there are tent exhibitions held in the open, but most of the tents on show will have nothing to do with backpacking! The typical modern tents are designed for camping holidays, and are more like canvas caravans or transistorized modern residences! Some manufacturers do specialize in making aerodynamic light-weight mountain tents with built-in ground sheets, and their advertisements can be seen in outdoor magazines.

The next most important item of equipment is the rucksack, which must of course be roomy as well as light.

Good modern backpacker sacks are designed to adjust to the body of the person and are framed, either outside or within the sack, so as to spread the weight to the pelvis instead of wholly on the spine. Here again it is a matter of trying it on to get the one that suits you best. It is not possible to give recommendations apart from a general note or two. Choose a large bag; larger than you think you might need – to take in at least 60 litres capacity. It should have the means to adjust in several ways to your back; also a large flap at the top. A separate bottom compartment that can be opened from the bottom is useful: that is where I usually keep tent and sleeping-bag. Detachable side pockets are handy. Fastenings should be quick-release. Shoulder-straps and other contact points should be padded. Zips should have flap protection. The total weight might be around two kilograms.

Next in order of importance is the sleeping-bag. My own is an old, but well cared-for, down bag weighing only 850 grams. This is fine in summer, but in winter, or in the mountains, I supplement it with an inner 'thermal' material liner weighing 480 grams. An insulated pad slips under the bag, and weighs hardly anything.

For cooking I have a little cooker which burns methylated spirits. I used to favour an efficient little paraffin pressure stove, but after a while I found it to be rather smelly. Meths I can live with, and the smell soon evaporates. The cooking pot goes as a good fit with the cooker, so there is no great loss of heat. The rest of the suggested gear is in Appendix 3. In total it should, say the experts, be not more than one third of your body weight.

Food has to be light-weight and that usually means no tinned goods, unless a small one like sardines. Good quality dehydrated is the stuff nowadays, but the cooking instructions need checking. Anything that takes more than fifteen minutes of cooking is going to use up fuel! Space also being at a premium, a container of oatcakes is better than bread.

There are plenty of books on mountaineering, only a few on backpacking. So I can recommend a slim book by Ken Ward, of the Backpackers Club: *Discovering Backpacking* is published by Shire Publications. The Backpackers Club should be joined by all who wish to backpack; it organizes courses; and it supplies a list of recommended sites for members.

There is a very special freedom in backpacking. You have everything about you that is needed to sustain life for an agreeably lengthened time. You have utterly cut away the bonds which tie you to civilization. You have food and shelter and a bed, and you can use it whenever you want.

HOSTELLING

Youth Hostels have no age restrictions, and good walking routes can be planned using hostels as en route inexpensive overnight accommodation. Membership is inexpensive. Hostels are meant for people on the move, with restrictions on the number of nights one can spend at each one. Beds should be booked well in advance after the walking route has been planned. You can choose to cater for yourself with the help of the hostel kitchen, or you can buy meals there. You may be asked to share some simple chores. Hostels vary as to what is on offer and they are far more luxurious than they used to be. Some are modest hotels with individual rooms, but normally one must share a dormitory. There are still some hostels in remote areas which can be quite basic, and some would prefer them that way.

The less gregarious like myself, with peace and quietness as an essential, might jib at the thought of what could be communal living. However, I must say that in my many hostel stays I do not remember feeling uncomfortable. You can meet interesting and pleasant company including overseas visitors, and not excluding the hostel wardens.

FARMS AND BARNS

Farmhouse accommodation offers a good option on many walking routes, and details of where and what is offered can normally be obtained from the local tourist offices which invariably guarantee a standard. Such accommodation offers a chance to meet real country folk with a very intimate knowledge of the areas. You may have to dine in the farm kitchen, though some provide modernized dining and living rooms. The food may be more than ample!

In some areas, particularly in National Parks, barns may be on offer as 'stone tents' with very basic amenities which should however include washing and toilet facilities. They may have to be booked at the park authority's office.

'B-AND-B'

A tourist office's list of bed-and-breakfast accommodation is a help in planning walks covering several days. However, it is risky to depend on finding vacancies en route during the tourist seasons, even in some remote areas. It may be necessary to get to the village where beds are on offer by 4 o'clock, and even then one might have to hike around to find a vacancy. Many walkers take a chance, as I have done, and have been lucky; but at holiday times, particularly during school holidays, the advice should be that it is far better to book accommodation in advance and use it as a base.

The Ramblers Association issues a book to members listing places specifically offering accommodation for walkers.

15

Enjoying the Countryside – The Gentle Art

It happened in a moment. It seemed that I held the moment for a while, and it was over. I was walking along a lane and stopped to look over a hedge. The ground fell in folds below, across a rough meadow with a lone ash tree, to the curve of a reed-fringed river, its running the only sound to break the silence. Beyond that the land sloped upwards past a second meadow with rock outcrops to a hedge-fringed country road, then to hillside holding a long band of mixed woodland. Behind in hazy distance were hills. I took in the whole. It was a pleasing scene well worth a stop to enjoy, but my attention was drawn to something high in the hedge: a single wild rose. Each time I looked at the scene I was drawn repeatedly to that pale red rose until it compelled and absorbed my whole attention. It was more than a rose, it was a statement. It stood between me and the clear sky, and though it appeared delicate and fragile it seemed for a brief moment to have the clear voice of authoritative conviction. It demanded attention; though it spoke in a language that I strained at, and failed to understand, yet somehow the effort gave a muted pleasure. I looked again at the scene spread beyond the rose and it was all the more significant, as if the flower was a necessary intermediary – like Chorus in a Greek play.

I suggested earlier that everything we might see in nature could have a mystical as well as a physical meaning. Of course I will allow that many may consider this is nonsense. Flowers only speak to poets. And if you are not interested in poetry you may think as I once did (and not yet totally convinced otherwise), that most poets are people who, if not totally mad, have by their nature to be hovering precariously on the verge.

But anyone who visits the countryside must at some time

150

or other have a similar experience. I shall always remember one small incident. I was once in charge of a party of prisoners from a local open prison engaged on a conservation task. One talkative character, an amiable and not very bright recidivist, thoroughly urbanized from an inner city, had attached himself to my side and was telling me all his troubles when a small tortoiseshell butterfly landed on a thistle directly in front of him. He stopped talking in mid-sentence; his mouth dropped open and at last, after an exclamatory expletive, he said, 'Will you look at that!' For just a second or two we shared the wonder of it; and then the butterfly was away and he eventually managed to take up the tale where he left off.

Surely, sooner or later in the countryside something grabs and gives your attention a good shake. It may be a whole scene or a feature in it. And it has a message, otherwise why does it make its demand? It captures like a snatch of music, saying something that moves feelings but is beyond comprehension. Normally one might dismiss the experience at once, and forget it like a brief inexplicable twinge of a nerve. We are practical people. As a result of our education and our long-practiced reactions we are governed by the dominant left hemisphere of the brain which deals wholly with the logical practical business of living.

But the gentle art of enjoying the countryside must involve that part of imaginative experience which is the realm of the right hemisphere of the brain; which is concerned with imagination, rhythms, patterns and creativity, and which is so strong in children, but by adulthood is too often weak from lack of exercise. But we all to some extent have the gift of imagination. Imagination holds our hopes and dreams, it gives life significance. Without it the often harsh realities of existence would be unbearable.

To appreciate nature to the full in a journey through the countryside needs an opening up of all the senses. But it also needs a journey through imagination; and the use of that inherent ability to recognize rhythms and patterns. For a while we may focus our attention on one point, maybe a

151

tree, which has enjoyable significance. In itself it can be an object of wonder; but if the attention is expanded to a realization that the tree could only be where it is, that it fits well into its chosen place, and then beyond that to the environment it shares with other plants, we may see that there is a peaceful gathering. Like a swarm of individual notes blended into music, every object forms part of a whole which is greater than the sum. Where there is a wholeness, there is peace.

To enjoy the gentle art of country walking to the full, we should have an interest in the natural world. But imagination must stretch to gather in its wholeness. If, in looking at nature, we are focusing and confining our study of one detail for too long; if we are only concerned with giving each plant, each bird and animal a name, it is helpful in their future recognition but it is not enough.

We can of course, as often in nature study, go far until it becomes an intellectual exercise, thus missing its enjoyment. We can be obsessed with collecting, dissecting, measuring, classifying, naming and recording until a stage is reached where nature is reduced to a dull and dusty formula. We can specialize until we reach that stage where we learn more and more about less and less. What can a man who only studies a drop of water know about the living, flowing river?

To enjoy what we see, to enhance our experience of a country walk, we need to go beyond detail to reach into imagination, and move at least some way to an understanding of the part that each living thing that we see plays in the great all-embracing web of life. Everything – from the most primitive of life forms to the elephant – has a cosmic significance. Every organism is an integral part of the great biological process.

We must go further. We should not walk as strangers into the natural world. The plants, the birds, the trees, the animals – all are fellow captives in the colossal net of life. We should recognize that we are a *part* of all that we see, not superior to it. At last we are beginning to understand that try as we may to pretend otherwise, we do not have a unique

152

and privileged relationship to the living world. We *belong* to it. It owns us. If the whole of humanity was to destroy itself tomorrow, taking with it the entire elaborate structure which has supported its survival, the heart of the natural world would hardly miss a beat. Life in its myriad forms could manage very well without us.

So when we walk into the countryside, we should be aware that we are inseparably a part of its life and it is a part of us. We are wrapped around with the perfect wholeness. And a touch of humility does nothing to harm the enjoyment of it. We might even feel some reverence . . .

So to walk; and you have left behind the old world and have come into the real world, and if you potter along the lane, or breast the hill, you may come to feel that what you thought were the important things – work, career ambition, the rivalry and competition, finance, status, the social group, the trappings of towns – all these fall into a new perspective. You may not be able to escape them for ever, but now, for a time, as feet stride out the rhythm you are free.

'The soul of a journey,' said William Hazlitt, 'is liberty, perfect liberty; to think, feel, do, just as one pleases.' Liberty is following one's own bent. Not being pressured to fill an alien role, but walking loose to the world.

Liberty in a country walk is a feeling that you have climbed out of the narrow confinement of daily routine. It is to abandon an obsession with '*life style*', and to begin to care about living.

But more than that. Country walking offers us the opportunity to be better than we are, physically, knowledgeably and spiritually. Open the door – stride out – and we have come home to the countryside where, in our heart's core, we all belong.

Appendix 1

LONG-DISTANCE PATHS
The established long-distance routes have not specifically been designated for the use of marathon walkers. Nor need they be walked along their whole lengths; they can be done in a choice of sections to suit ability and taste.

Expect to see waymarking signs, but map-reading skills will almost certainly be needed!

'Long distance' is freely interpreted. Some are relatively short, but are included here as they were established to offer routes of special scenic or historical interest.

As this goes to press, new routes are still planned and the list cannot claim to be comprehensive.

England and Wales: ('National Trails' waymarked with an acorn symbol)

The Pennine Way. Edale to Kirk Yetholm. 250 miles (402km).

The Cleveland Way. Helmsley to Filey. 93 miles (150km).

The Pembrokeshire Coast Path. Amroth to Cardigan. 186 miles (300km).

Offa's Dyke Path. Chepstow to Prestatyn. 168 miles (270km).

South Downs Way. Eastbourne to Winchester. 106 miles (171km).

South West Coast Path. Minehead to Poole (through Somerset, Dorset, Devon and Cornwall in four sections). 562 miles (904km).

Ridgeway. Overton Hill to Ivinghoe. 85 miles (137km).

North Downs Way. Farnham to Dover. 141 miles (227km).

Wolds Way. Filey to Hessle. 79 miles (127km).

Peddars Way and Norfolk Coast Path. Thetford to Cromer. 93 miles (150km).

New routes to be established include Hadrian's Wall, and a Thames Path.

Countryside Commission guide books are available from bookshops or from Countryside Commission Publications, 19/23 Albert Road, Manchester M19 2EQ.

There are other long-distance routes linking rights of way which are not national trails; these have been detailed by individuals and organizations and shown in local guide books.

Scotland: (waymarked with thistle symbol)

The West Highland Way. Milngavie to Fort William. 95 miles (153km).

The Southern Upland Way. Portpatrick to Cockburnspath. 212 miles (341km).
Information leaflets from the Countryside Commission for Scotland, Battlebly, Redgorton, Perth PH1 3EW.

The Speyside Way. Spey Bay to Glenmore. 60 miles (97km). Leaflets from Moray District Council, District Headquarters, High Street, Elgin.

Official guide books on Scottish Long-Distance Routes are on sale at bookshops.

Ireland:

The Western Way. Westport to Oughterard. 45 miles (73km).

Sli Ulaidh (Ulster Way, Donegal). Donegal to Falcarragh. 40 miles (65km).

The Cavan Way. Blacklion to Dowra, Co. Leitrim. 16 miles (25km).

The Leitrim Way. Dowra to Glenfarne (to link with the Cavan Way). 18 miles (29km).

The Tain Trail. Circular from Carlingford. 19 miles (30km) with 3,600ft (1100m) of ascent.

Grand Canal Towpath. Dublin to Shannon Harbour. 81 miles (130km).

The Dublin Way. Jobstown to Shankill. 25 miles (41km).

Slieve Bloom Way. Circular round the Slieve Bloom mountain range. 31 miles (50km).

The Wicklow Way. Marlay Park to Clonegal, Co. Carlow. 81 miles (130km).

South Leinster Way. Kildavin, Co. Carlow to Carrick-on-Suir. 58 miles (93km).

Munster Way. Carrick-on-Suir to the Vee, on borders of Co.'s Tipperary and Waterford. 40 miles (65km).

The Kerry Way. Killarney to Glenbeigh (to be extended). 35 miles (57km).

Sli Chorca Dhuibhne (The Dingle Way). Dingle Peninsula, Tralee to Dingle. 28 miles (45km).

The Kildare Way. Celbridge to Edenderry. 46 miles (74km).

Information from Bord Failte, Irish Tourist Board, Ireland House, P.O. Box 273, Dublin 8, *or* Irish Tourist Board, Ireland House, 150 New Bond Street, London W1Y 9FE.

Northern Ireland:

The Ulster Way. Around Northern Ireland (still under negotiation but sections available). 435 miles (700km).
Information from The Sports Council for Northern Ireland, House of Sport, Upper Malone Road, Belfast BT9 5LA.

Isle of Man:

The Millennium Way. Ramsay to Castletown. 21 Miles (34km).

Raad Ny Foillan (The Road of the Gull). Coastal path round the island from Peel. 90 miles (145km).

Bayr Ny Skeddan (The Herring Way). Castletown to Peel. 14 miles (22½km).

Brochures and maps obtainable from Isle of Man Tourist Information Office, Douglas, Isle of Man.

Appendix 2

The Ramblers Association,
1/5 Wandsworth Road,
London SW8 2LN.
Founded 1935. The major organization which seeks to protect and promote rights of way and access to open country. Has branches and affiliated clubs throughout Britain.

Open Spaces Society,
25a Bell Street,
Henley on Thames,
Oxon RG9 2BA.
Founded 1865. Seeks to protect and promote legal access to common land in England and Wales. (Over 1.5 million acres; 510,000 ha. over which there is legal access to only 25 per cent.) Concerned with the protection of rights of way.

Scottish Rights of Way Society,
John Cotton Business Centre,
10/12 Sunnyside,
Edinburgh EH7 5RA.
Founded 1845. Promotes preservation, maintenance and defence of public rights of way in Scotland.

Backpackers Club,
20 St Michael's Road,
Tilehurst,
Reading RG3 4RP.
The organization catering for backpackers. Organizes meets and training sessions. Publishes magazine *Backpack*.

British Mountaineering Council,
Crawford House,
Precinct Centre,
Booth Street, East,
Manchester M13 9RZ.
Represents the interests of mountaineers, rock climbers, and fell walkers. Concerned with access to hills and climbs, with conservation issues, with training.

Mountaineering Council of Scotland,
9 Ilay Court,
Bearsden,
Glasgow G61 1RT.
Has the same interests as above, for Scotland.

Cospoir,
The National Sports Council,
Hawkins House,
Dublin 2.
Concerns itself with the footpath systems in Ireland and works on a commendable network of marked paths throughout the republic.

The Sports Council
16 Upper Woburn Place,
London WC1H 0HA
Aims to foster sport and recreation amongst the general public. A channel for funding of projects.

HOSTELS AND COUNTRY HOLIDAYS ASSOCIATIONS

Irish Youth Hostels Association (An Oige),
39 Mountjoy Square,
Dublin 1.

Scottish Youth Hostels Association,
7 Glebe Crescent,
Stirling FK8 2JA.

Youth Hostels Association,
Trevelyan House,
St Albans,
Herts AL1 2DY.

Countryside Holidays Association (C.H.A.),
Birch Heys,
52 Cromwell Range,
Manchester M14 6HU.
Walking holiday centres in country houses.

H.F. Holidays Ltd,
Imperial House,
Edgware Road,
London NW9 5AL.
As above.

Farm Holiday Bureau,
National Agricultural Centre,
Stoneleigh,
Kenilworth,
Warwickshire CV8 2LZ.
Has network in Britain of farming families offering country
holidays.

CONSERVATION SOCIETIES

British Trust for Conservation Volunteers,
36 St Mary's Street,
Wallingford,
Oxon OX10 0EU.
The organization which has teams of volunteers working on
conservation projects throughout England, Wales and
Northern Ireland. Welcomes new recruits and runs train-
ing programmes.

Scottish Conservation Projects Trust,
Balallan House,
24 Allan Park,
Stirling FK8 2QG.
Has the same aims as above, covering Scotland.

Association for the Protection of Rural Scotland,
Charlesto,
Dalguise,
Nr. Dunkeld,
Perthshire PH8 0JX.
Aims to protect the Scottish countryside.

The Council for the Protection of Rural England,
Warwick House,
25 Buckingham Palace Road,
London SW1W 0PP.
Founded 1926. Supports and promotes legislation for protecting rural land, and keeps a watchful eye on threats to it. Has local branches.

Campaign for the Protection of Rural Wales,
Ty Gwyn,
31 High Street,
Welshpool,
Powys SY21 7JP.
As above, in Wales.

Friends of National Parks,
Council for National Parks,
246 Lavender Hill,
London SW11 1LJ.
Support group for Council for National Parks which was set up as Standing Committee on National Parks in 1936 as a grouping of organizations largely responsible for the eventual passing of the National Parks and Access to the Countryside Act of 1949 for England and Wales. Seeks to make public more aware of the parks and to promote improved legislation.

Friends of the Earth,
26–28 Underwood Street,
London N1 7JT.
A leading environmental pressure group and watchdog in the United Kingdom. Has network of local groups. Sets up and promotes environmental projects. Member of Friends of the Earth International which has groups in thirty-eight countries.

Friends of the Earth (Scotland),
Bonnington Hill,
72 Newhaven Road,
Edinburgh EH6 5QG.
Same aims as above, for Scotland.

Greenpeace,
Greenpeace House,
Canonbury Villas,
London N1 2PN.
Stated aim: to promote peaceful but uncompromising action in defence of the environment.

International Tree Foundation.
Sandy Lane,
Crawley Down,
West Sussex RH10 4HS.
Promotes the planting and protection of trees internationally, but local groups promote tree-planting schemes in Britain.

John Muir Trust,
Gardenhurst,
Newbigging,
Broughty Ferry,
Dundee DD5 3RH.
Campaigns for the protection of the wilder regions of Scotland while respecting the well-being of those who live in them.

The National Trust,
36 Queen Annes Gate,
London SW1H 9AS.
Founded 1895. The leading charity in England, Wales, and Northern Ireland which seeks to acquire, preserve, and sometimes improve, property for the benefit of the general public. Now a major landowner.

The National Trust for Ireland (An Taisce),
The Tailor's Hall,
Dublin 2.
Founded 1948. Ireland's leading conservation society which promotes the care of Ireland's countryside, wildlife and historic sites by ownership and by promoting new legislation.

The National Trust for Scotland,
5 Charlotte Square,
Edinburgh EH2 4DU.
Founded 1931. Scotland's leading charity with similar aims to the National Trust above.

R.S.N.C. Wildlife Trust Partnership,
The Green,
Nettleham,
Lincoln LN2 2NR.
Founded 1912. The national association of Britain's County Naturalists' Trusts which have local membership and own many nature reserves, and concern themselves with nature conservation generally. Publishes magazine *Natural World*.

Royal Society for the Protection of Birds,
The Lodge,
Sandy,
Beds SG19 2DL.
Founded 1889. Promotes protection of birds and owns nature reserves. Has local groups. Publishes magazine *Birds*.

Scottish Wildlife Trust,
Cramond House,
Kirk Cramond,
Cramond,
Glebe Road,
Edinburgh EH4 6NS.
Concerns itself with the conservation of wildlife and habitats in Scotland.

Transport 2000,
Walkden House,
10 Melton Street,
London NW1 2EB.
Campaigns for transport policies that will benefit the public while not harming the environment.

Wildfowl & Wetlands Trust,
Slimbridge,
Glos GL2 7BT.
Owns several bird reserves and promotes knowledge of and interest in birds.

The Woodland Trust,
Westgate,
Grantham,
Lincs NG31 6LL.
A charity which seeks to acquire broad-leaved woodlands as they become available, and protects and manages them.

OFFICIAL AUTHORITIES

The Countryside Commission,
John Dower House,
Crescent Place,
Cheltenham.
Glos GL50 3RA.

The Countryside Commission for Scotland,
Battleby,
Redgorton,
Perth PH1 3EW.

Countryside Council for Wales,
Plas Penrhos,
Ffordd Penrhos,
Bangor,
Gwynedd LL57 2LQ.

Department of the Environment,
2 Marsham Street,
London SW1P 3EB.

Department of Highways, Ports and Properties,
Sea Terminal,
Douglas,
Isle of Man.

National Parks and Monuments Service,
Office of Public Works,
51 St Stephen's Green,
Dublin 2.

TOURIST AUTHORITIES

English Tourist Board,
Thames Tower,
Black's Road,
London W6 9EL.
and
123 Lower Baggot Street,
Dublin 2.

Irish Tourist Board (Bord Failte),
PO Box 273,
Dublin 8.
and

150 New Bond Street,
London W1Y 9FE.

Isle of Man Tourist Board,
Douglas,
Isle of Man.

Northern Ireland Tourist Board,
59 North Street,
Belfast BT1 1ND.

Scottish Tourist Board,
Croythorn House,
23 Ravelston Terrace,
Edinburgh EH4 3EU.

Wales Tourist Board,
Brunel House,
2 Fitzalan Road,
Cardiff CF2 1UY.

Appendix 3

RECOMMENDED FIRST-AID KIT
(Per person or small party – expand for larger party.)
3-inch elastic bandage
1-inch (25mm) roller bandage
2-inch (50mm) roller bandage
Small sterile wound dressing
Large sterile wound dressing
three triangular bandages
Several sizes adhesive plasters ('Bandaids')
    or one 'cut your own size' roll
Small pair scissors
Six safety-pins
Small pack paper tissues
One or two pairs plastic disposable gloves
Tweezers
Needle
Book matches
six paracetamol tablets
six antacid indigestion tablets
Glucose tablets
Sun cream
Lip salve
Insect repellent

Appendix 4

WEATHER FORECASTS
Dial 0898/500 followed by the regional code, any time of
day or night.

MOUNTAIN WEATHER

Western Highlands 0898 500 441
Eastern Highland 0898 500 442
Lake District National Park, Windemere (05394) 45151
Snowdonia National Park, Llanberis (0256) 870120

Appendix 5

RECIPES

Elderflower champagne (non-alcoholic)
three large heads of elderflower
1 gallon water
one large lemon
1½ lbs cane sugar
2 tablespoons of white vinegar
Mix and stir all the ingredients except the lemon. Squeeze in the lemon. Cut the rind into large pieces and add. Leave all to steep for twenty-four hours. Strain and pour into screwtop bottles and store in a cool place for a fortnight before use.

Sloe gin
About 1lb of sloes (picked end of October)
1lb sugar
one bottle gin
Prick each sloe with a fork. Half fill bottles with the sloes, add equal quantity of sugar. Pour on the gin to almost fill the bottles. Store. Invert the bottles regularly to mix in the sugar.
(Just about ready for Christmas and New Year.)

Index

R.S.P.B. 163
Rucksack 23, 24
  backpacking 146, 147
Ruskin, John 144

Scotland,
  Mountaineering Council of 159
  Scottish Conservation Projects Trust 161
  Scottish Rights of Way Society 158
  Scottish Tourist Board 166
  Scottish Wildlife Trust 164
Sea shore 115 et seq.
  tides 115, 116
  natural history 116, 117, 118
  birds 119, 120
Socks 11
Sports Council 159
  Ireland 159
Sticks, walking 28, 29
Stream side 121, 122
Survival bag 136

Transport 2000 164

Wales Tourist Board 166
Walking clubs 72, 73
Walking pace 34, 51, 52, 72
Walking, rhythm 69, 70
Walking, solitary 77, 78
Walls 92
Ward, Ken 147, 148
Waterproofs 17 et seq.
  'breathables' 21
  cape 18
  cotton, close weave 21, 22
  cotton, waxed 22
  colour 19
  light-weight 18
  over-trousers 19

THE SHINING LEVELS

John Wyatt

The Shining Levels is John Wyatt's classic account of throwing up his job in the city and getting a job as a forest worker in the Lake District. Going back to nature was never more vividly described. This is a story of hardships as well as joys, and of his developing friendships with the local characters and with Buck, an orphaned faun.

'A delight for all those who love nature.'

DAILY MIRROR

'The story of a man who went back to nature; funny, instructive and a rare treat.'　　　SUNDAY TIMES